DQ80

**Making
the City
Observable**

Richard Saul Wurman

Published by
Walker Art Center
Minneapolis, Minnesota
and
The MIT Press
Cambridge, Massachusetts
and London, England

Richard Saul Wurman is the
third specialist to participate
in the Walker Art Center/Graham
Foundation program in design
criticism.

Mr. Wurman's collaborators:
Don Moyer
Ephraim Matthew Miller
Nancy Donovan

Four photographs from the center of the intersection at 13th
and Arch Streets in Philadelphia,
looking north, east, south and
west. The set is part of a series of
photographs documenting inter-
sections.

Table of Contents

Note

Quotation marks indicate descriptive material has been taken from the cited publications.

Mr. Wurman's comments are set in italics.

This issue of Design Quarterly ex-
plores some of the existing data
systems which describe, in visual
terms, various urban entities:
transportation systems, roadways,
public buildings, land patterns,
historical structures, as well as
some new methods for developing physical information that
will be widely used in the future.
Through these means the individual acquires information about his
surroundings.

A citizen who understands the
highway system and its relationship to the other urban systems—
housing, transportation, business,
schools—has a basis for making
decisions regarding highway expansion, elimination of cars from
core areas, and linkage of the highway system to various means of
public transportation. Where do
people live relative to their work,
to nature, to leisure time activities? Is our city protecting and
using its natural resources in an
intelligent way? How does the
park system relate to the schools,
to residential cores, to the larger
geographical complex? This issue
of Design Quarterly contains
some of the materials designed to
elucidate the city and examines
the possibilities of enlarging
the scope and increasing the avail-
ability of public information.
The material shown here is, of
necessity, only an initial look

at what is available; it is in no
sense meant to be exhaustive.

Similar materials could be the
basis, in every city, for the development of what Richard Wurman
calls an "urban data center," for
the dissemination of information
related to the public environment.
To dispense information on a day
to day basis, one might begin,
with a school-based facility, to
develop pertinent data on local
surroundings. This small system
could be linked to a large central
information core that would
gather material from localized
centers and combine all available material into an information
system to describe the total area
on a large scale, thus creating an
"urban observatory."

Design Quarterly is grateful to
the many publishers and individuals who lent materials for
reproduction here; they are all
designated along with the materials described. We are indebted
to Don Moyer, of Murphy Levy
Wurman, who gathered and prepared the information along with
Mr. Wurman. The generous
assistance and interest of
Mr. Michael Connolly, Editorial
Director of The M.I.T. Press,
has made it possible to enlarge
this issue to its present size and
scope.

MSF

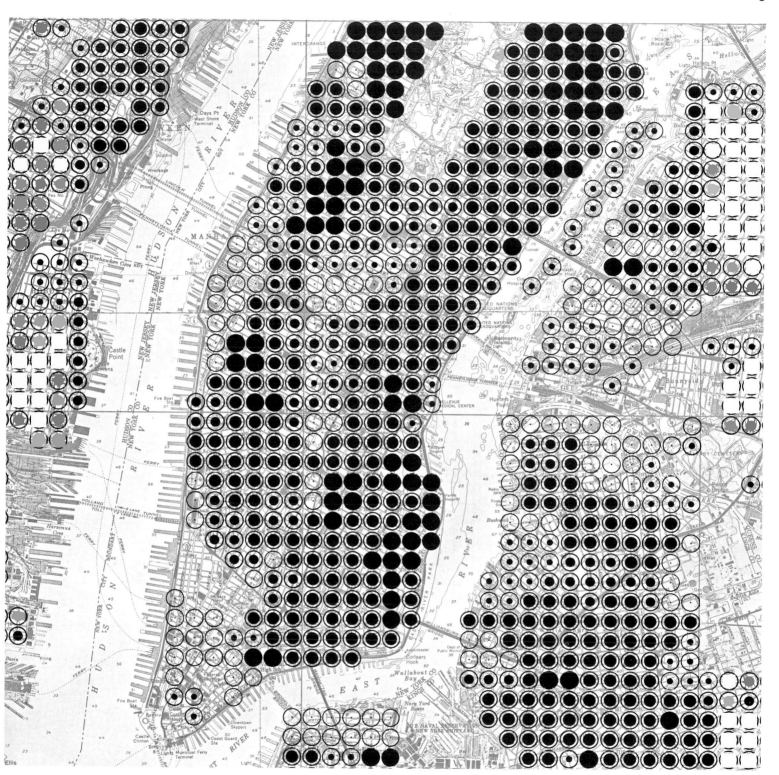

detail actual size from
New York City **The Urban**
Atlas see pp 24—25

Public information should be made public.

Information about our urban environment should be made understandable.

Architects, planners and designers should commit themselves to making their ideas immediately comprehensible.

p 68
p 33
p 54
p 83
Making the city observable implies allowing the city to become an environment for learning. The city can be made observable by developing a school curriculum about our man-made environment, by designing a clear subway map or by producing a ballot that people can understand and use intelligently.

Some approaches that clarify the urban scene:
The New York Times illustrated the moon landing of Apollo 14 with maps and diagrams clearer than any ever used to describe the location of a new highway on earth.

Burlington Industries invites the public to see a capsule version of all their activities in their Avenue of the Americas offices in New York.

CBS-TV in New York City has a new program,"The Urbanites," that gives specific information about what is happening in the city.

ABC took a full page ad to translate an election ballot into understandable English.

The book, **Cosmic View, The Universe in Forty Jumps,** shows the universe minified and magnified in scale changes to the power of ten, and provided the basis for Charles Eames' remarkable p 22 film, **The Powers of Ten.** Both book and film attempt to show the scale relationships among elements we perceive and among those we only conceive of.

In the 17th Century Jan Blaeu drew maps of all the towns in the Netherlands locating each house clearly and accurately.

Mayor John Lindsay has proposed a special zoning district for Fifth Avenue; he suggests that at least the first two floors of each building be retail or public service spaces, instead of allowing the invasion of the ground floor by anonymous, uninteresting office buildings and banks.

In contrast to the above:

We talk in numbers we can't comprehend and about sizes we can't visualize. p 85

Artists' renderings, rather than measured performances and relationships, are used to explain proposed environmental changes.

A twelve year old child gets lost downtown.

A visitor speaking a foreign tongue feels helpless in the subway. p 54

A voter votes for bond issues to finance unexplained projects.

A school board spends millions and incurs endless debts building new schools to house an educational system which they all agree to be increasingly unworkable, hostile and irrelevant to the world around it.

A local transit authority is losing money yet it cuts back service and raises fares, insuring fiscal disaster. The emperor has no clothes!

Why don't we have chartbooks and understandable data describing our cities? p 62

An urban **The Way Things Work.** p 61

Why doesn't every community have a community map? p 77

Why can't there be pocket guides to every city?

Why not paint the streets in a way that will make the city a life-sized route map? p 88

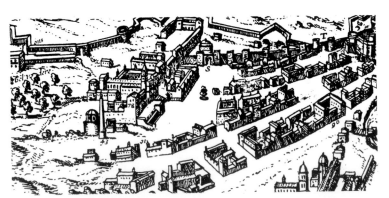

Actual size detail from
Civitates Orbis Terrarum
plan of Rome

p 84 Why don't industries intimately involved with our cities use their advertising to educate the public in the areas of their concern?

p 66 Why isn't the city a schoolhouse?

Why does a young student learn Latin and logarithms by rote instead of learning to understand his environment through direct experience?

p 74 Why don't we use the tops of our tall buildings for observing the city and educating our young?

p 82 Why don't in-flight films orient you to your destination?

Why can't TV news programs report daily happenings in the streets, focusing attention on the publicly owned sector of our cities?

Why are we unable to discern the patterns of the movement systems we are immersed in continuously?

How do we describe spaces and places?

How do we describe and notate paths, directions and routes?

How can each of us articulate our ideas and encourage the expression of the demands and ideas of others?

DQ 80 is a collection of gestures toward solutions.

I've included those projects that are close to my particular experience. Many come from books in my library or from people I know. The projects represent both ideas and dreams as yet unfulfilled as well as items available on local newsstands and bookstores. Most are visual. Many contain the spin-off of ideas and techniques applicable to the educational and political problems that engulf us.

Everything we do is education. The city is education but the architecture of education rarely has much to do with the building of schools. The city should be a schoolhouse and its ground floor can be both bulletin board and library. If we can make our urban environment comprehensible, observable and understandable we will have classrooms with unlimited windows on the world.

The city should offer students experts who share their concerns, and diverse, free and exciting spaces and places in which to have learning experiences. There are many ways to make the city observable. A walk through the city's ground floor should be a continuous learning experience.

As we are all students we should be concerned about real experiences and situations independent of books, classrooms and school buildings.

We should develop skills and abilities for communicating information about the environment both verbally and visually.

We should create the kind of confidence in a student that will enable him to judge and develop criteria that might be used in the evaluation or creation of his own environments.

We should understand that ecology includes the total physical environment, public and private, not simply the problems of water and air pollution.

We own one-half of the land p 91 in our cities yet our concern is only with the appearance, not even the performance of the other half.

Architects and planners have been participating in a marathon contest to expand the physical form of our cities—pitting one extruded building against another—gaining support for highly styled packages that misrepresent their contents and ignore their neighbors.

Most experts in city signage somehow never discuss communications, only graphics.

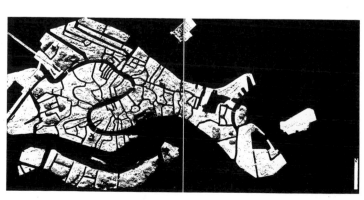

Detail of
The city of Venice model
from **City Form and Intent**

Transportation engineers talk
of movement in terms of actual
speed, rather than of psychologi-
cal time, comfort, safety, orientation and information.

In our race to invent facades we
have overlooked the need to
make clear our performance
goals. Designers have become
urban beauticians applying mas-
cara and calling it beautification,
building urban Edsels and calling
them street furniture.

The limited amenities an individual can afford when he lives
in isolation are multiplied by
thousands when he lives in a
community where collective
amenities are possible, including
facilities for:
     free and convenient
     movement of all kinds,
     the opportunity to pur-
     chase goods and services,
     protection and shelter,
     orientation, learning and
     guidance.

If the patterning, disposition
and performance of these facilities are made clear, the city is
then observable.

Making the City Observable is a
catalogue of projects, ideas,
books, guides, maps, advertisements, and curricula that offer
some means to a better understanding of the environment.
Making the city observable
means making the plethora
of public information public.

This issue of Design Quarterly
is about education. Education
is about communication, and
communication at its best is
both an art and an entertain-
ment. A catalogue gives a pro-
vocative hint of items and ideas
available. This catalogue
attempts, through the juxtapo-
sition of some eighty projects,
to outline a syllabus for urban
communication.

Population Graph—Map, U.S.A.
Laboratory for Computer
Graphics and Spatial Analysis

Richard Saul Wurman

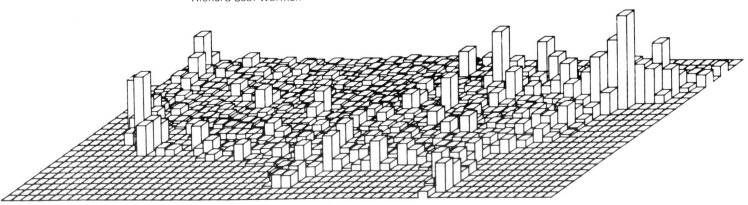

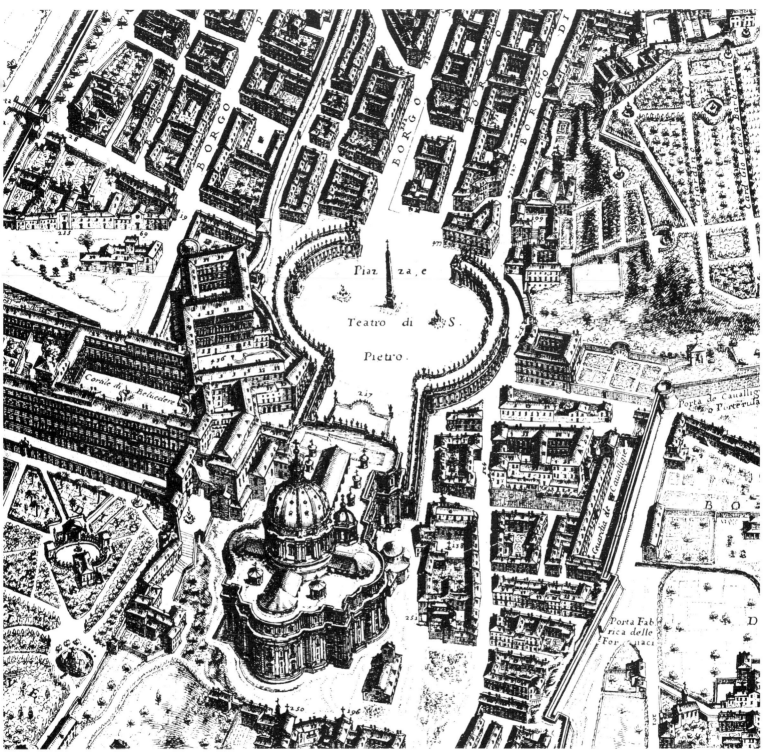

Vatican area of Rome.

The 12 page Falda Plan of Rome was drawn and incised on copper by Giovanni Battista Falda in 1676 with revisions added in 1756 and 1864. The original materials are preserved in archives in Rome.

The maps include all the streets, squares, churches, important public buildings, and gardens of Rome and an index with the exact names of all entries.

The perspectival elevations produce an extremely clear visualization of the city.

This lead entry is representative of several items that follow— pictorial maps from the bird's-eye that show the plan and the look of a city, building by building. The scale is instantly apparent because of familiar objects that are notated throughout.

Falda's Plan of Rome
Giovanni Battista Falda
1676
M. Danesi
56″ x 56″
90 DM ($24.75)
Available from:
Wasmuth Buchhandlung und Antiquariat
Hardenburgstrasse 9a
Berlin 12, Germany

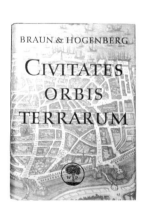

". . .published in 6 volumes from 1572 to 1617 and remains the most original and magnificent of all city atlases. Its compilers were the first to apply the systematic atlas form, devised by Ortelius, to a collection of plans and views, that is, in the field of chorography. . ."

"Throughout the Middle Ages towns had been represented in profile, as seen from the ground, with emphasis on conspicuous or important buildings. . . In the middle decades of the 16th century however geographers, surveyors and engineers introduced geometrical methods of mensuration enabling smaller areas, as in a map, to be delineated from a vertical viewpoint. So the town-plan was reborn, and it quickly became recognized as the only form of topographical representation in which spatial relationships were correctly expressed and the structural growth of a city, in terms of history and geography, could be discerned."

"The **Civitates** was the first serious attempt to give graphic representation of the main cities of the world, with a wealth of factual detail." In all six volumes (three books) 546 cities and towns are represented.

"In the main the buildings in each view are shown in elevation, and while the ordinary dwellings are stylized, the principal buildings are reproduced from actual drawings on the spot, and these, and the main streets, can be recognized today. Further, the editors gave additional factual information as a deliberately planned policy, such as the heraldic arms of the city, and the nature of the surrounding countryside, whether wooded or arable, grazing land, vineyards or gardens. The importance of waterways is stressed by the careful delineation of stone bridges, wooden pontoons, flat-bottomed ferries, moles, wharves and jetties; the ports with ocean-going craft, the inland waters with river traffic. Varieties of land travel are depicted: pedestrian, horse, wagon, coach and palanquin.

Small vignettes illustrate the trades, occupations, and habits of the locality. The law is represented by various forms of punishment: gibbet, wheel, whip, etc. A distinctive feature of the plates is the insertion of large figures in the foreground to illustrate local costumes."

Published in facsimile these three volumes are exceptional. The introduction is an excellent history of the project and as one looks through these plates he is continually reminded that the view consistently taken by the cartographer was one he could never see. The desire to be as a bird and see the city spread out before you in order to clarify the information is evident. The plates also show costumes of the day and are filled with many fantastic ideas of places perhaps never seen. The intent of the books to create a comparative atlas of world cities has yet to be matched or equaled.

Civitates Orbis Terrarum
Braun and Hogenburg
1572 — 1618
1966
three volumes
12'' x 17 1/2''
$200.00
World Publishing Company
2231 West Tenth Street
Cleveland, Ohio 44102

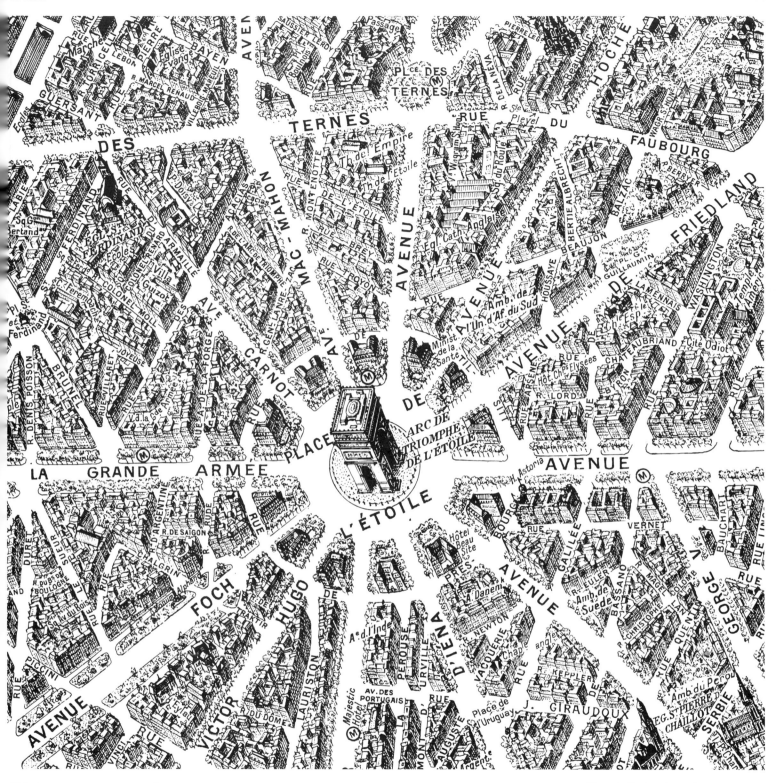

This is a more recent example
of a pictorial plan and is there-
fore more rigorously developed
from an accurate plan. It is
handsome, available and would
be more useful as a guide to
Paris were Metro stops, etc.,
more assertive in their notation.

Plan de Paris a Vol d'Oiseau
G. Peltier de 1920 a 1940
1959
two sheets
200 x 160 cm, or 74 x 104 cm
60.00 francs ($10.92)
Libraire Blondel la Rougery
7 rue Sainte-Lazare
Paris 9e, France

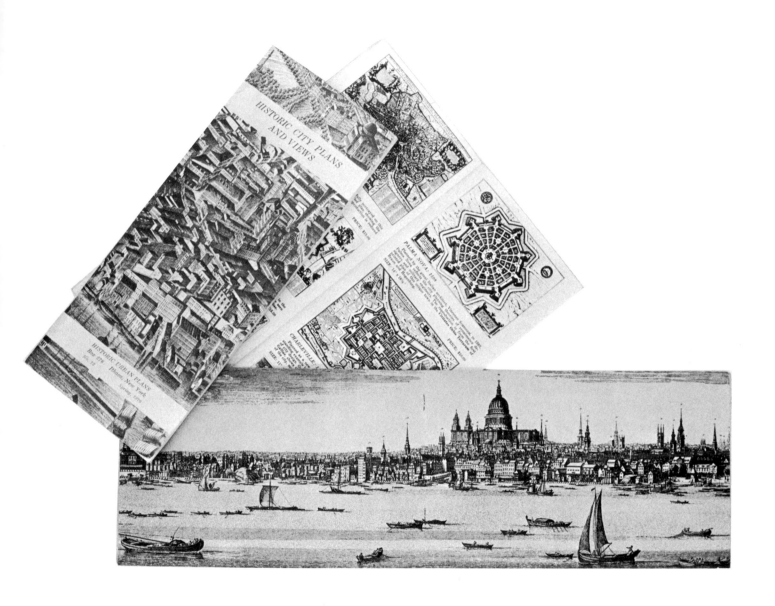

Moderately priced reproductions
of historic urban plans and views,
each an authentic plan significant
in the history of city development,
are available from Historic Urban
Plans. Plans of London include
general views and panoramas as
well. The listing is arranged in
chronological order from the six-
teenth century to the end of the
nineteenth century.

*The two free catalogues list
plans available for purchase.*

Historic City Plans and Views
54pp catalogue
5'' x 12 1/2''
free
Historic Urban Plans
Box 276
Ithaca, New York 14850

Plans of London
9 1/2'' x 6''
free
Weinreb and Douwma
39 Great Russell Street
London WC1, England

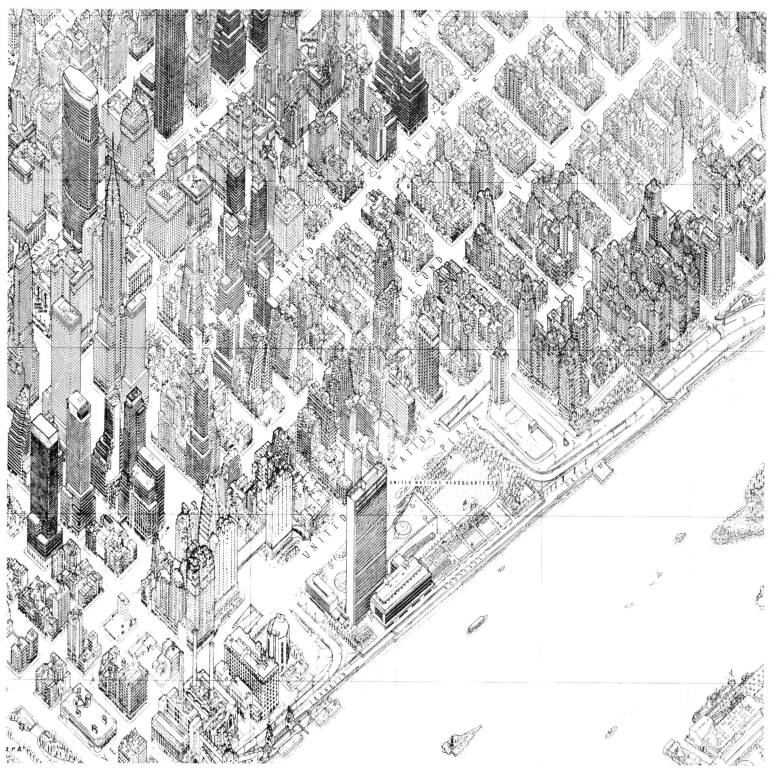

Because of his love for architecture, Herman Bollmann, a graphic designer from Braunschweig, Germany, walked and drove the streets of 23 cities making drawings and in 1948 translated them into appealing personal graphics.

Today, automatic aerial cameras and camera-furnished cars provide the data used by professionals as basic material for drawing these maps. The maps are updated periodically to include recent

buildings and show, through clear, reliable comparisons, the development of a city. Twenty-five of these city picture maps are collected in the first book "Städte" (Cities). The Bollmann series now includes over 100 city maps. 117 European cities and New York City.

This is the most energetic modern day version of the Civitates Orbis Terrarum. These maps are accurate, complete and fascinating and allow the pursuit of the city building by building. Most of his over 100 cities are in Germany, Netherlands, etc., although Bollmann has produced an incredible New York City (shown here) and one on Jerusalem.

Herman Bollmann
Faltausgabe: DM 4,10-5,50
Buttenplan, plano: DM 8,-16
Bollmann Bildkarten Verlag
Richterstrasse 5
Braunschweig, Germany

Palmanova

"This is a collection of photos of clay models of fifty significant towns and cities all to the scale 1:14,400."

"The list of cities is simply those locations that I am familiar with and that to me give forth an immediate positive image."

Aigues-Mortes, Amsterdam, Angkor, Assisi, Athens, Avila, Babylon, Bern, Bruges, Cambridge, Chandigarh, Chartres, Chichen-Itza, Carcassonne, Granada, Hook, Karlsruhe, Kristiansund, Lucca, Lübeck, Machupicchu, Middelburg, Miletus, Montagnana, Monte Alban, Mont-Saint-Michel, Moscow, New York, Nördlingen, Palmanova, Paris, Peking, Pergamum, Persepolis, Philadelphia, Pompeii, Portofino, Priene Pyramid Complex, Rome, Saarlouis, Sabbioneta, San Gimignano, Savannah, Siena, Tikal, Timgad, Venice, Versailles, Washington, D. C.

"The plates that form the basis of this issue were produced on 108 separate squares of masonite each 16" on a side. The models were built from white plasticene, balsa wood and paint. They were done to the scale 1:7200-600 feet to an inch and photographically reduced to 1:14,400-1200 feet to an inch. The models were produced largely by the efforts of Professor Wurman's second year studio in architecture with help from other members of the student body. They were photographed by Ralph Mills from the visual aids department and reprocessed by Eugene Feldman, owner of the Falcon Press in Philadelphia.

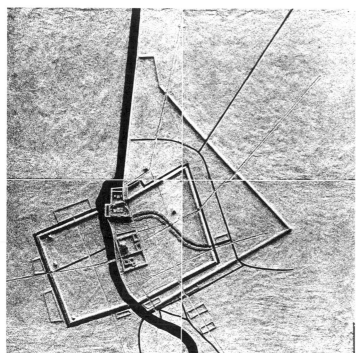

Babylon

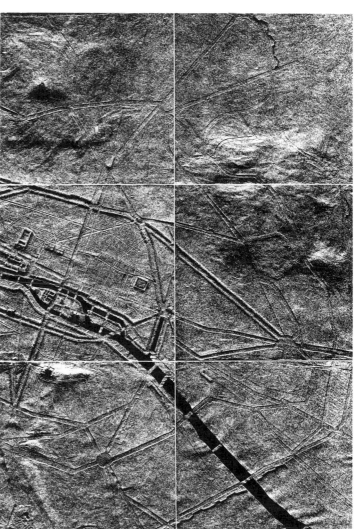

Washington, D. C.

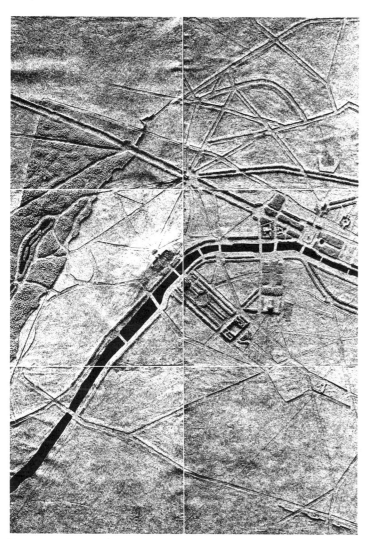

Paris

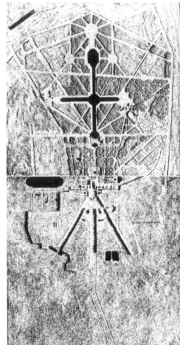

Versailles

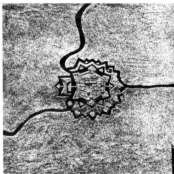

Saarlouis

Peking

As one only understands relative to something one already understands the idea of comparison is basic. The plates show little information except for the gross form characteristics of each city and although the quality of analysis is uneven the volume collectively has been received well.

I would like to redo this book with overlays of additional data.

City Form and Intent
Richard Saul Wurman and students
1963
50 plates
8 1/2'' x 8 1/2''
out of print
Student Publication
The School of Design
North Carolina State University
Raleigh, North Carolina 27607

"This photomosaic depicts complete global coverage assembled from pictures taken during 12 consecutive orbits on October 31, 1966, by the ESSA III meteorological satellite."

These photographs are used in preparing daily worldwide meteorological analyses and forecasts. The camera system was in a circular orbit at a 750-mile altitude.

Exploring Space with a Camera
Edited by Edgar M. Cortright
National Aeronautics and
Space Administration
1968
214 pp
9" x 11 1/4"
$4.25
U.S. Government Printing
Office Bookstore
710 North Capitol Street
Washington, D. C. 20402

from **Exploring Space with a Camera**

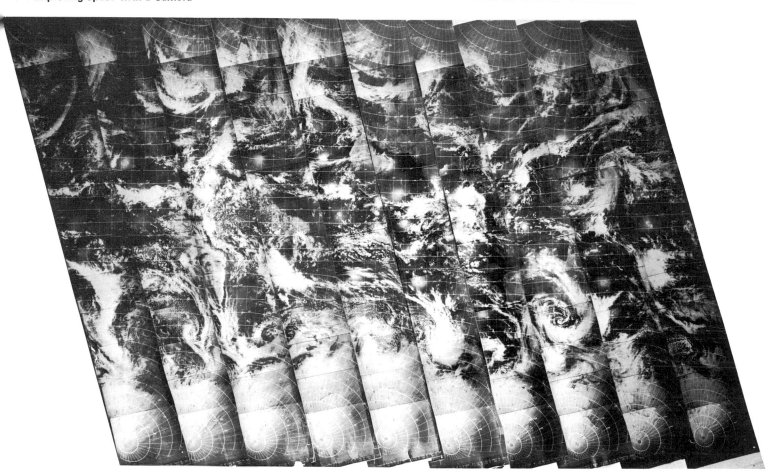

Airborne Camera
Beaumont Newhall
1969
144 pp
8 3/8" x 10"
$10.00
Hastings House Publishers
10 East 40th Street
New York, New York 10016

Atlas Aerien
Pierre De Fontaines and
Mariel-Brunhes Delamarre
1962
tomes I — V
8 1/4" x 10 3/4"
$8.50 each
Wittenborn & Co., Inc.
1018 Madison Avenue
New York, New York 10021

Europe from the Air
Emil Egli and
Hans Richard Muller
1959
223 pp
9" x 11"
out of print
George G. Harrap & Co. Ltd.
182 High Holborn
London WC1, England

Europe: Aerial Close-up
Charles E. Rotkin
1962
221 pp
10" x 13 3/4"
$6.95
Crown Publishers and
Bonanza Books
419 Park Avenue South
New York, New York 10016

Aerial photographs are available from the government and from private companies. Both vertical and oblique photographs may be ordered from their files. The U.S. Geological Survey publishes an index map periodically to show the status of aerial photography. Photographs obtained by the Geological Survey, except those subject to security restrictions, are generally for sale to the public. The Canadian National Air Photo Library has a program

which makes it convenient to order aerial photographs of a specific area for as little as $.60.

Photographs by Aero Service

These two views of Levittown, before and after its construction, clearly indicate the change that has occurred in the landscape.

Map Information Office
U.S. Geological Survey
Washington, D. C. 20242

National Air Photo Library
Surveys and Mapping Branch
Department of Energy, Mines
and Resources
615 Booth Street
Ottawa 3, Canada

Aero Service
4219 Van Kirk Street
Philadelphia, Pennsylvania 19135

SYMAP (Boston), which has been developed at the Laboratory for Computer Graphics of Harvard University, generates maps of spatially distributed data which are located according to pre-determined base map positions. The program uses combinations of the standard computer printout symbols to achieve white-black tone range which corresponds to a low-high data value range. In order to identify place units more easily the maps used in this report are produced with an acetate overlay showing the principal roads and shoreline of the study area; the original map size was 32" x 24".

Dr. Carl Steinitz
Assistant Professor of City
Planning and Landscape
Architecture
Harvard Graduate School
of Design
Laboratory for Computer Graphics
and Spatial Analysis
Graduate School of Design
Memorial Hall 121
Harvard University
Cambridge, Massachusetts 02138

See page 26

New Haven census study.

Ross Hall
Census Use Study
U.S. Department of Commerce
Bureau of the Census
Washington, D. C. 20233

Population distribution in the United States in 1960 shown in isometric diagram based on county statistics (U.S. census) population aggregated into one-degree quadrilaterals of latitude and longitude. This provides an empirical two-dimensional "signal" which can be analyzed in terms of the expected signal suggested by geographical theory. A nonlinear vertical scale of population is used in the graph for better visibility. The diagrams were produced on a Cal Comp Model 763 Zip Mode plotter and Model 780 off-line tape unit.

Dr. Waldo R. Tobler
Associate Professor of Geography
Department of Geography
University of Michigan
Frank Rens
Graduate Assistant

Rain patterns on 60 square mile area in east-central New Jersey on 28 November 1966.

Sol Dworkin
Head, Educational Programs
and Exhibit Department
Bell Telephone Laboratories
Mountain Avenue
Murray Hill, New Jersey 07974

Charles Eames is one of those rare, particular people. This film is a collection—not unlike this DQ—of projects that describe the city. The second half of the film is the better part and it is scenes from that half that are reproduced here. They are generally representative of the more technical visual means being used to describe urban related phenomena.

Thermogram measuring the city's emitted infrared radiation recording degrees of heat as different colors.

John E. Hurley
Barnes Engineering Company
30 Commerce Road
Stamford, Connecticut 06904

In 1968 Governor Terry Sanford requested that a study related to the most populated area of North Carolina, nominally the Urban Crescent, be initiated through the newly created State Film Board. The end product was to be a cogent description of this twelve county area, aimed to educate the citizenry of the State to enthusiastic acceptance of a regional planning body, which was to be created. The theme of the film is the growth of the twelve Piedmont Counties from 1850 to the year 2000. These counties are initially set in the context of the State of North Carolina, then the southeastern region of the U.S., the eastern U.S. from the Mississippi River, and the entire U.S.

Richard Saul Wurman
Murphy Levy Wurman
Architecture and Urban Planning
1214 Arch Street
Philadelphia, Pennsylvania 19107

False color—remote sensing residential area.

Duane F. Marble
Remote Sensing Laboratory
Department of Geography
Northwestern University
Evanston, Illinois 60201

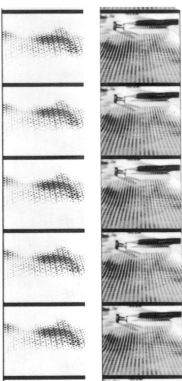

Assortment of symbols
Urban Atlas
20 American Cities

see page 24

right:

Emergence and Growth of an Urban Region
By Constantinos A. Doxiadis

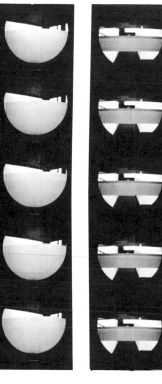

NASA Houston Space Center
color graphics

Peter Kamnitzer
Urban Laboratory
School of Architecture and
Urban Planning
University of California
Los Angeles, California 90024

See page 23

Traffic loading study

Ev Merritt
Bureau of Public Roads
Federal Highway Administration
U.S. Department of Transportation

Animated sequence of the 1965
northeast blackout. Based on
information provided by
Westinghouse.

Nine-lens view of New York City
Coast and Geodetic Survey's
nine-lens mapping camera de-
flects the images from eight of
the lenses through mirrors to form
this flower-petal design.
Joined by special rectifying
equipment into a single wide-angle
picture, the images produce an
undistorted plan view of the city
in which the street grid is square,
while the tall buildings are flared
out by perspective.

U.S. Coast and Geodetic Survey
9000 Rockville Pike
Bethesda, Maryland

right:
Model showing land value
and population density for
a computer demonstration of
city planning simulation.
By Eames office for IBM.

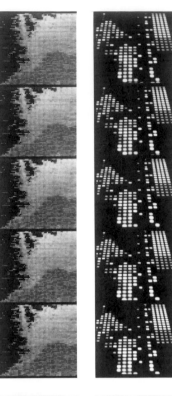

Nimbus Earth Resources
Observations
Project NERO

In an experimental IR tracking
technique, a radiometer in Nimbus
II, a NASA weather satellite,
senses the sharp boundary between the 75° F. Gulf Stream
and cooler waters. A computer
calculates temperatures for five
mile-square areas, and an optical
device converts them into a
color-enhanced mosaic. It shows
land as green, cool water as
yellow, warmer ocean as red.
Splotches south of the boundary
are clouds, shown in blue. Future
satellites might read 200-foot
squares and pick up sub-surface
temperatures from instrument-
carrying buoys, thus yielding
heat maps useful for navigation.

James R. Greaves
Manager
Geophysical Space Sciences
Allied Research Associates, Inc.
Virginia Road
Concord, Massachusetts 01742

Tornado isodensitracer. Isodensi-
tometric trace of a portion of a
photograph of tornado activity
in which the quantized output
of a microdensitometer is coded
into a repeating series of symbols.
When a set of scans is automati-
cally completed, the contours of
equal photographic density are
readily recognizable.

Brian J. Thompson
Ronald H. Johnson
Technical Operations,
Incorporated
Technical Operations West
441 North Whisman Road
Mountain View, California 90404

Earthquake prediction pictured
left is a four hundred mile
wide section of southern California and northern Mexico
around the San Andreas Fault.
These computer printed patterns indicate lines of constant
energy in the earth's crust.
This application computes
changes in elastic energy and
pinpoints locations where earth-
quakes are most likely to occur.

Willem J. van de Lindt
IBM Scientific Center
10889 Wilshire Boulevard
Los Angeles, California 90024

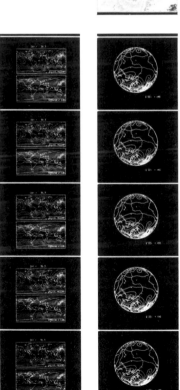

Weather simulation. This is a
weather map of weather that
never happened, at least not in
the real atmosphere. It is taken
from a single frame of a compu-
ter-produced movie that shows
changing sea-level pressure
patterns of computer-generated
weather that "happened" only
in the electronic circuits of
NCAR's Control Data 6600
computer system.

Henry H. Lansford
Public Information Officer
Dr. Akira Kasahara
Project Head
National Center for
Atmospheric Research
P. O. Box 1470
Boulder, Colorado 80302

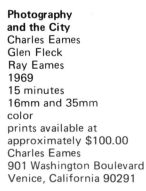

**Photography
and the City**
Charles Eames
Glen Fleck
Ray Eames
1969
15 minutes
16mm and 35mm
color
prints available at
approximately $100.00
Charles Eames
901 Washington Boulevard
Venice, California 90291

Powers of Ten
Office of Charles Eames
1969
10 1/4 minutes
16mm and 35mm
color
prints available
for $125.00
Charles Eames
901 Washington Boulevard
Venice, California 90291

"Given that the physical environment is not in perfect harmony with every man's life style, given that architecture is not the faultless response to human needs, given that the architect is not the consummate manager of physical environments, I shall consider the physical environment as an evolving organism as opposed to a designed artifact. In particular, I shall consider an evolution aided by a specific class of machines. Warren McCulloch (1956) calls them ethical robots; in the context of architecture I shall call them architecture machines."

Grope and Stare are eyes for the architectural machine. Grope (illustrated) is a low resolution sensor with a retina composed of an array of photocells which can be sampled individually by the machine. Sampling its environment digitally, Grope can only tell the machine "yes" or "no", "I see light" or "I do not see light".

Inputs to Stare pass through an analog-to-digital convertor and are separately addressed as eight bit inputs.

GROPE is an $18.00 Japanese toy tank with sixteen photocells mounted on it. Since the construction of the original GROPE by Steven Gregory, two further GROPES have been built to investigate tactile inputs. One gropes through, bumping into limiting boundaries or obstacles; the

other samples horizontal surfaces for texture discrimination.

Decisions are made on the available evidence, but future and stronger evidence may contradict a previous 'probably.' A heuristic program must not only recuperate from the 'bug,' but its subsequent decisions must be improved by the 'experience' of the error.

In addition to giving our machine visual channels into the real world, two added benefits accrue from studies in machine vision. First, the heuristics of recognition appear to be very close to the heuristics of classification. In other words the way we see things may map directly into how we employ these images. The recognition of commonalities in patterns, intentions in forms, and perhaps meaning in architecture may be related to the heuristics, even semantics, of recognition. Second, not only does heuristic programming have an obvious use in machine vision, it has a still more significant and unexplored potential in computer-aided design. After all, the handling of initial design concepts is a matter of 'probably this, probably that.'

In low-resolution vision experiments, the inputs are restricted to a maximum of twenty-four photocells or photovoltiac cells. As a result discrimination can only be achieved by making the interface more active than in the high-resolution case. The eye must become an actuator: moving in order to affect the patterns on its own retina and observing the resulting changes and its behavior in response to these changes.

As an analogy, consider the problem of selecting the toy in a toy store that is the most fun for a five-year-old child. One method would be to list all the variables involved, their interrelationships (to the best of our knowledge), and the so-called utility function

(or parameters of maximization). A computer program might be able to consider all the combinations for this relatively simple problem, but even here, because of missing information and misinterpreted and misused (context-dependent) information, it probably would come up with a mediocre answer. A second method, one we believe to be more appropriate, is to send a five-year-old child into the store and simply ask him to play with the toys. By observing his behaviour, it will be obvious which toy of those he has played with is the most fun.

It is in this vein that we handle low-resolution vision. We give the device a role as opposed to a goal; looking as opposed to recognizing. Then we, or another machine, as an onlooker, follow the behaviour of the device and extract information from its behaviour rather than from the scene itself.

GROPE, 4 and STARE, 3 are two examples of such devices; each has a retina composed of an array of light-sensors which can be individually sampled by the machine. The retina can, for example, be actuated to move or rotate for the purpose of reexamining the status of its photocells. This technique can deal with moving objects, with major delimiting lines in a scene, and with large bodies of constant tone.

INTUVAL (Intuition and Evaluation) is a computer graphic program utilizing interactive computer graphics (IBM 360/91 and 2250 display scope) for systematic evaluation and iterative refinements of intuitively conceived design proposals. Presently INTUVAL uses a simple transportation model for evaluating some of the physical and socio-economic repercussions of alternative freeway routes. Evaluations for six parameters and several subcomponents each are displayed on line in bar chart form. A simplified impact model generates before-after land value maps on-line. Trade-offs between major parameters are not internally performed but are left to the decision makers. The program is intended for designers and for non-expert user-participants.

Architecture Machine
Nicholas Negroponte
1970
153 pp
7 3/8" x 7 3/8"
$5.95
The M.I.T. Press
50 Ames Street
Cambridge, Massachusetts 02142

INTUVAL
Peter Kamnitzer
School of Architecture and
Urban Planning
University of California
Los Angeles, California 90007

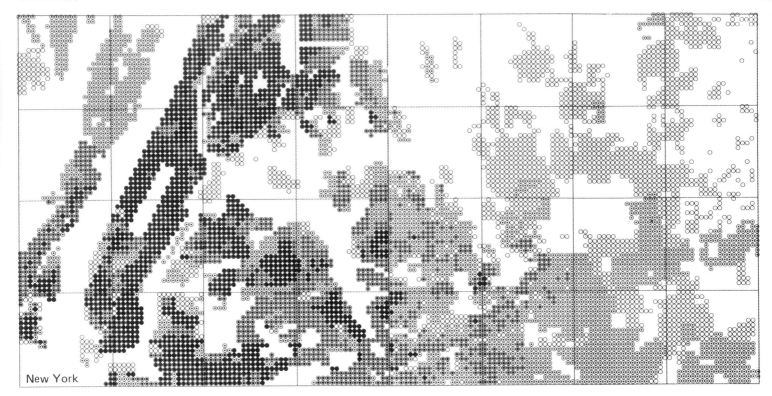

New York

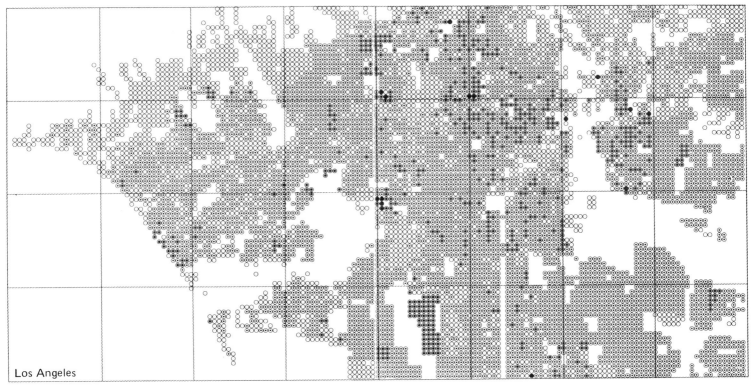

Los Angeles

Maps of twenty urban regions, all at a scale of 1:48,000. "This book is a preliminary investigation of visual systems of programming information for metropolitan-scale design. For our purposes there exist three major categories of urban information: (1) the nature of the people, (2) the nature of the land and its uses, (3) movement of people, goods, and information. These maps all describe (1) classifications (or type) of things or events,

(2) their magnitude, (3) their location in space and time."

"Comparable data mapped at the same scale for a number of cities are useful because unfamiliar situations are best described and understood by comparison with familiar situations. Accurate and complete information about most urban phenomena is difficult to amass, and comparative information is now almost unobtainable."

"The information in this atlas (population, density, income intensity, and land use) is fundamental to an understanding of city form, but it was selected also simply because it was available."

"All of this information (1) is comparable by class, magnitude, and location, that is, the relationships (or non-relationships) of dissimilar urban phenomena can be studied directly; (2) is here organized visually; but (3) has

been also organized systematically and mathematically and can be factored, aggregated, projected in time, and reproduced by automated methods."

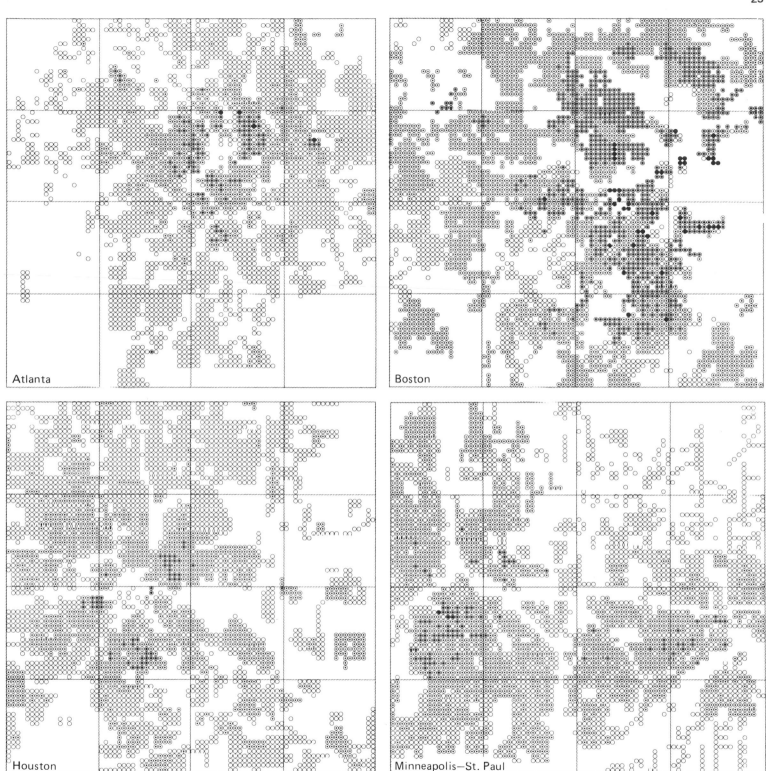

Atlanta

Boston

Houston

Minneapolis—St. Paul

These maps show population densities relatively and comparatively. There exists no standard scale or ledger used by American cities to describe themselves. There is no visual summary of U.S. Census information. This book hinted at solutions to the above.

Urban Atlas: 20 American Cities
Joseph R. Passonneau and
Richard Saul Wurman
1968
135 plates and introduction
17 1/2'' x 17 1/2''
$100.00
The M.I.T. Press
50 Ames Street
Cambridge, Massachusetts 02142

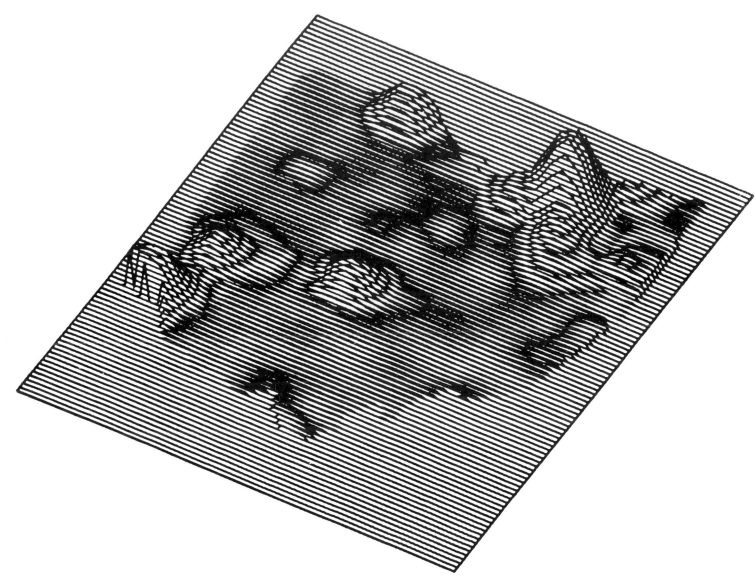

". . .the Laboratory has developed programs for high speed electronic digital computer mapping and new techniques for graphic display that utilize the accuracy, thoroughness, speed, and low cost of computers."

The Laboratory's past work in graphics was built largely on the computer mapping program developed at Northwestern University's Technological Institute by Howard T. Fisher. The technique, called the Synagraphic Mapping System, or SYMAP, is capable of composing spatially-distributed data of wide diversity into a map, a graph, or other visual display.

The second type of research undertaken by the Laboratory is pure research in the framework of general systems theory and spatial patterns. Much of the spatial analysis research constitutes work in what might be called "general spatial systems" theory, undertaken in relation to architecture, landscape architecture, city and regional planning, and urban design, with emphasis on the roles of computers in programming, design, simulation, and evaluation.

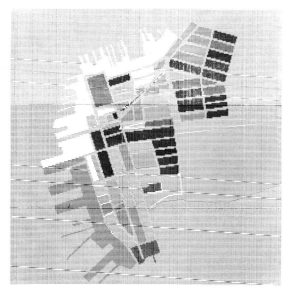

East Boston Recreation Study

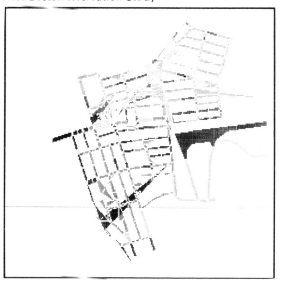

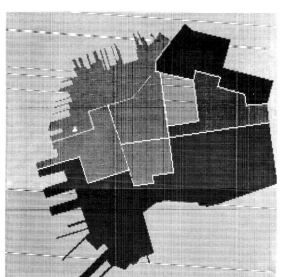

*The Laboratory was known for
some time for its major program,
SYMAP, but has more recently
branched out into many different
programs, some of which are
shown here. Their looseleaf
ring binders of programs are cer-
tainly worth purchasing.*

Manhattan Low Income Study

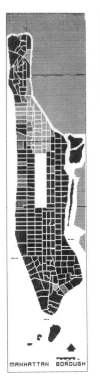 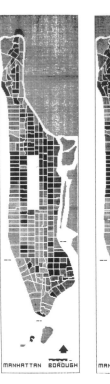  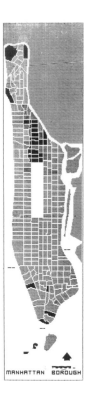  

Boston industry and
traffic flow diagrams

 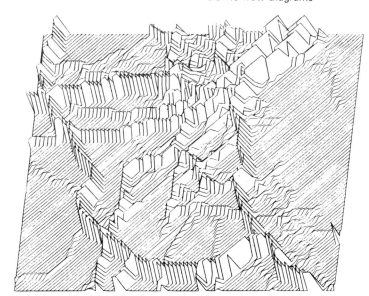

**Laboratory for Computer Graphics
and Spatial Analysis**
200 pp
8 1/2" x 11"
$12.00
Graduate School of Design
Memorial Hall 114
Harvard University
Cambridge, Massachusetts 02138

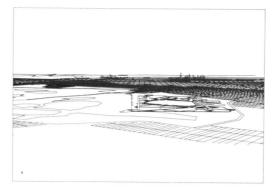

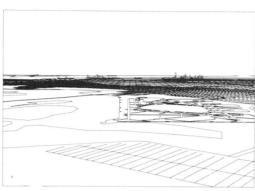

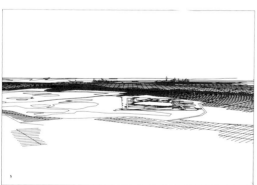

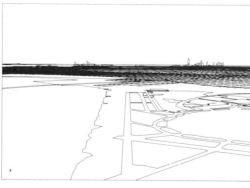

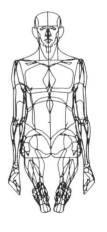

William Fetter who was supervisor of the Computer Graphics Division of Boeing has been involved in the production of many different projects of great fascination.

The two shown above are: the landing at an airport in a computer generated film, and a computer drawn man which has been used in a number of films at Boeing, and in this case, commercially for Norelco. Designed

for use in man-machine interaction studies, the measurements of the man represent the man-measurement of 50 percent of Air Force pilots, based on anthropometric data.

William Fetter used the animated figure data he created at Boeing through arrangements with Computer Graphics Inc.

William Fetter
705 North Oakland Avenue
Carbondale, Illinois 62901

**Computer Graphics
in Communication**
William Fetter
1965
128 pp
6'' x 9''
$4.95 hardcover
$3.50 softcover
McGraw-Hill
330 West 42nd Street
New York, New York

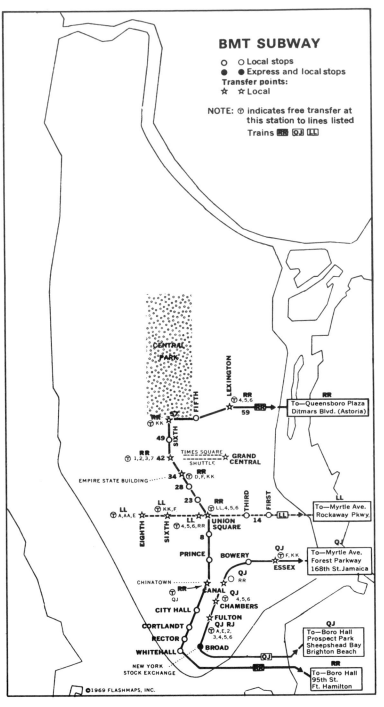

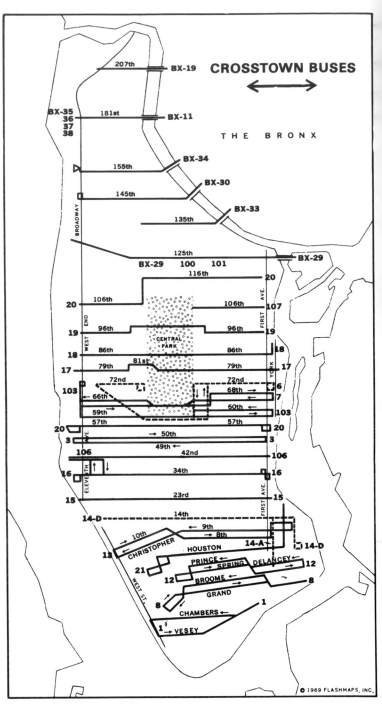

In this collection of 46 maps of the Borough of Manhattan, the maps are essentially similar in basic grid, but each is marked with a single category of useful information. One map, for example, shows only crosstown bus lines, another uptown buses. There is also a simplified "Address Finder" and a list of emergency telephone numbers.

A collection of well conceived, clear but not very elegantly produced maps of Manhattan, not of New York as the title implies. The clarity is based on the decision to separate each subway line on a map by itself and to separate cross town buses from uptown buses, etc. Each map gives one kind of information clearly.

New York in Maps
Toy Lasker and Jean George
46 flash maps
81 pp
4 1/2'' x 8''
$1.50
Flashmaps, Inc.
207 East 32nd Street
New York, New York 10015

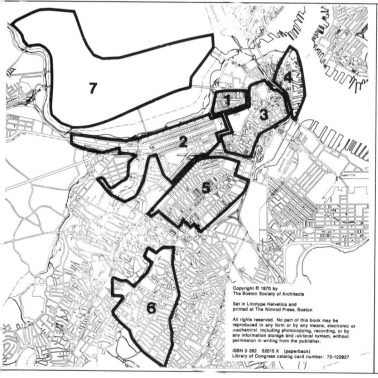

Contents

Originally prepared to introduce Boston to members of the American Institute of Architects meeting there in June, 1970, this guide is a thoroughly professional and handsomely presented handbook for the practicing architect, planner, or deeply interested layman. Organized by sections of the city, the book attempts to communicate the unique character of each, and to demonstrate their historic-architectural cohesion.

Boston Architecture is a finely produced guide of the seven sections of Boston oriented to architects. I fault this where I find fault with many other guides of this kind in that their photographs, although of high quality, have a tendency not to show buildings in context but buildings for buildings sake.

Boston Architecture
Edited by Donald Freeman
Boston Society of Architects
1970
122 pp
9'' x 9''
$2.95
The M.I.T. Press
50 Ames Street
Cambridge, Massachusetts 02142

1904 list of Baedeker's guides

Nord Amerika
Canada
Alps (Eastern)
Austria
Belgium and Holland
Berlin
Egypt
France (Northern)
France (Southern)
Germany (Northern)
Germany (Southern)
Germany (Rhine)
Great Britain
Greece
Italy
Italy (Northern)
Italy (Central)
Italy (Southern)
London
Norway, Sweden, Denmark

Palestine and Syria
Paris
Spain and Portugal
Switzerland
United States

Karl Baedeker
4 1/4'' x 6 1/4''
from $.90 to $4.80
originally published by
Charles Scribner's Sons

Nairn's Paris
Ian Nairn
1968
220 pp
4 3/8'' x 7''
$1.65
Penguin Books, Inc.
7110 Ambassador Road
Baltimore, Maryland 21207

Nairn's London
Ian Nairn
1966
272 pp
4 3/8'' x 7''
$1.95
Penguin Books, Inc.
7110 Ambassador Road
Baltimore, Maryland 21207

"This guide is simply my personal list of the best things in London. . . .What I am after is character, or personality, or essence. . . The book is organized into what seemed to be common-sense areas. Within them, the order does indicate a route of a sort; but this is not intended to be a package tour. . .Everything in the book is accessible. Locked churches are out unless the keys are freely given. . .This, quite obviously, is not a normal guide and is not trying to be one. If you want straightforward, general information, the best bet is probably the **Blue Guide**."

Nairn—As you can see from the above description this is a most personalized guide to a city and it is here listed as an example of just that.

Karl Baedeker was the turn of the century travel guide expert with no equal. I've listed here the books that he had available about 1904. Many of his guides are easily purchased, inexpensively, at used book stores. The one on the U.S., pictured open here, is particularly fun to read. I've used his books as supplemental guides on a recent trip to Europe and find them still quite informative.

Baedekers Paris
1909
454 pp, 52 maps
4 1/4'' x 6 1/4''

Baedekers United States
1904
660 pp
4 1/4'' x 6 1/4''

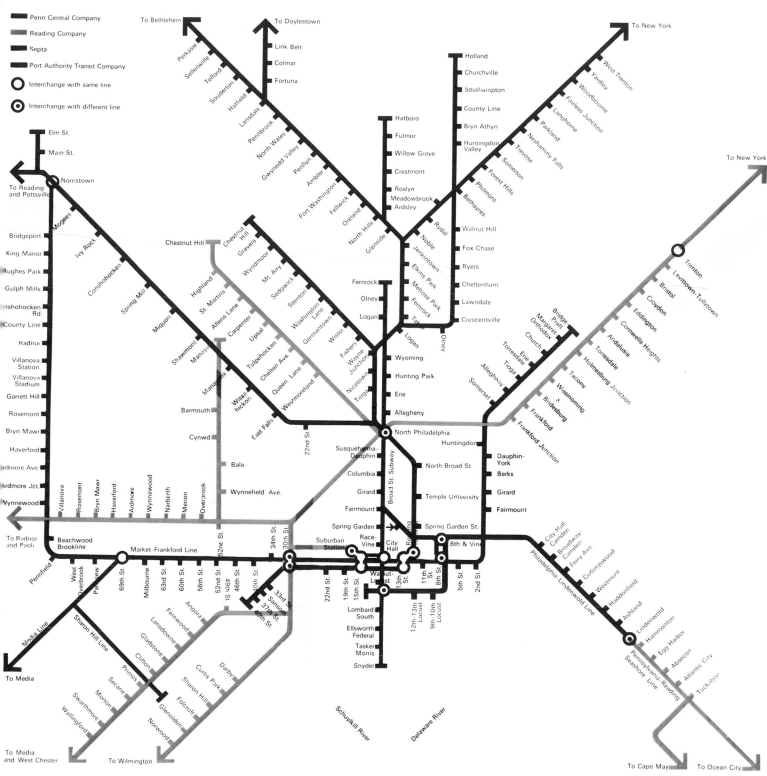

Subway and commuter rail map.
Original in colors.

Most cities have guidebooks describing the activities of the city, listing theaters, museums, restaurants, hotels, and special events of interest to tourists. For a few cities, there are guidebooks to their significant architecture. In both cases, activities and architecture are presented as objects within the city to be searched out and enjoyed.

This book does not try to duplicate traditional activity guidebooks. Rather, it is a guide to the urban environment of the city, organized and presented in a manner similar to the actual experience of the city by visitor or citizen. Most people view the city, as they move through it, either by car or on foot. The streets and walkways are the primary means of organization and are the areas from which the architecture of the city is observed.

Philadelphia is a city that has grown and changed over several hundred years. Its routes and areas are characteristic of many cities throughout the United States. The manner of presentation used in this text for Philadelphia should be applicable to all cities and the information presented has been selected with that in mind.

Map of area highway network—
related to map on previous page.

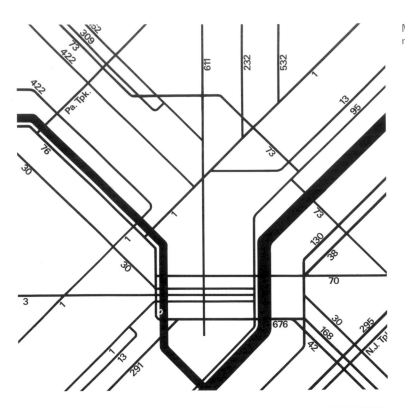

Center city map, typical of area
maps in the guide.

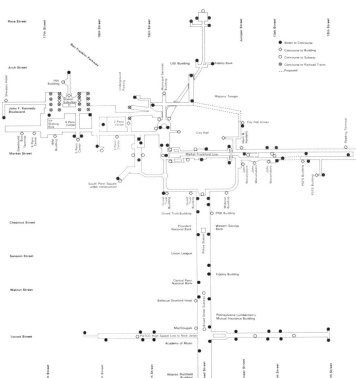

Underground concourse diagram.

Routes—Public streets are the primary determinants of the form of the city. They range in scale from expressways, to major arterial streets, to significant streets confined to a particular area of the city. Certain buildings stand out along the routes, either by position or architectural appearance, and usually serve as visual landmarks which help to identify specific places or characteristics of specific areas. The routes, and the physical environment along them, are the initial and dominant experience of the city for all people.

Areas—Housing, commerce and industry all expand along movement systems. These areas invariably touch on the major routes of the city and then grow out from them into fairly defined areas of consistent use. Within most cities, there are a limited number of areas of particular interest — downtown, universities, primary residential areas — each with its own architectural environment.

Demography and Geography—The routes and areas describe the city as it is today. But this present form is the result of development and change over long periods of time, and subject to a variety of influences — population expansion and movement, street growth and urbanization, regional transportation — all influence the present form of the city. This present form is, in turn, controlled through a series of legal and political districts which are designed to help it function and provide the complex range of services required by the population.

Plans and Planners—Present form and patterns of growth are generally the result of a limited number of consciously developed public policies and plans. Many cities have simply grown without any controls and the resultant form is dependent upon the network of streets. In all cases, the final achievement is the result of work by individual architects serving both the public and private clients in carrying out their objectives within the context of a broader image of the city.

Man-Made Philadelphia
Richard Saul Wurman and
John Gallery
96 pp
11″ x 10″
Available Spring 1971
Philadelphia Magazine
1500 Walnut Street
Philadelphia, Pennsylvania 19102

from: Guida Rapida of Touring
Club Italiano-authorized reproduction

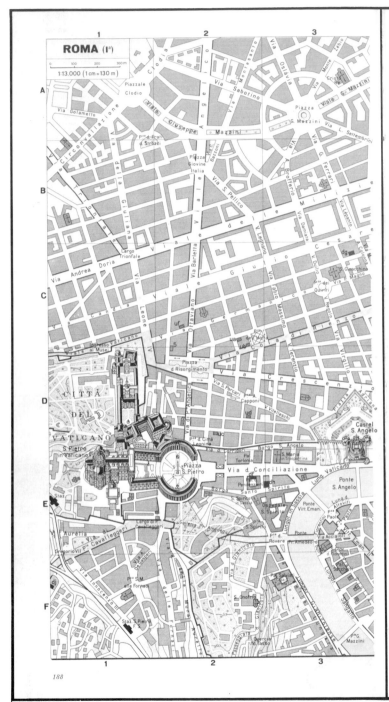

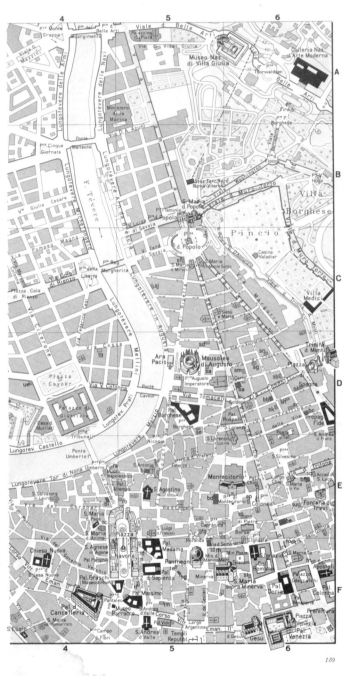

Touring Club Italiano has offices in 19 regions of Italy and offers its members a variety of publications for touring Italy and other areas of Europe. Guidebooks to 23 different regions of Italy contain detailed descriptive information about the people, geography, and culture of each area. There is a set of guidebooks with concise descriptions of 3 areas of Italy, as well as a set of similar brief guides to nine European countries. Routes are mapped out by the Club so that a reader can choose an area and the length of time he wants to travel by following the Club's guide. The Club offers guides to the mountains and seas of Italy and to its restaurants and hotels. One book describes the cooking of Italy; another two volumes, the sports in 2 areas of Italy. The Club also offers a variety of road maps of Italy and an archeological map.

Touring Club Italiano is Italy's answer to Michelin. They have produced a three volume guide to Italy which combines some of the aspects of Michelin's Green Guides and their standard red guide of France.

The maps of the larger cities rate significant buildings on a scale of annotation from coloring it a flat color to drawing it in perspective. They are clear and useable.

Touring Club Italiano Guides
270 to 344 pp
12,5 x 23 cm
4400 L to 5450 L
($7.04 to $8.80)
A83 Italia Settentrionale
A84 Italia Centrale
A85 Italia Meridionale
Touring Club Italiano
Corso Italia N10
20832 Milano, Italy

MIDTOWN MANHATTAN

SEE PAGES 82–153

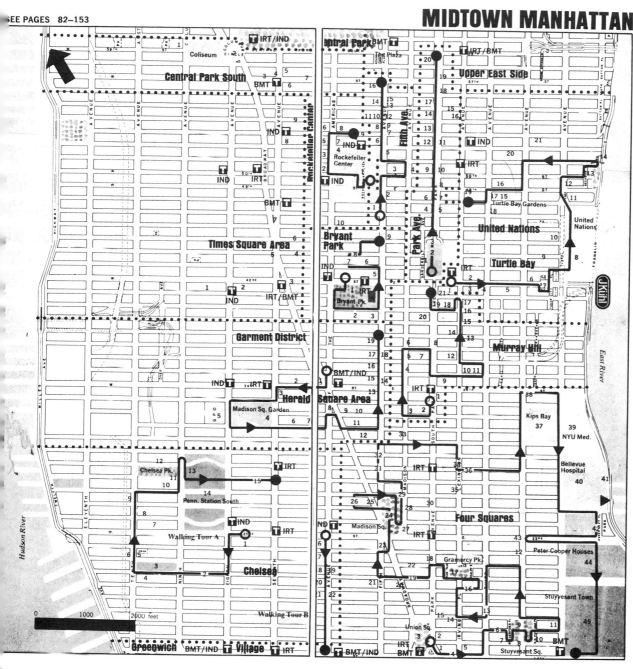

The guide is published under the sponsorship of the AIA, New York Chapter. Each of the five boroughs is discussed separately with its own maps, tour instructions, and individually numbered entries. Buildings, structures, streets, landmarks and parks are captured in photographs. There are more than 1500 entries, with informative descriptions.

The primary purpose of this book is to indicate, by way of thousands of examples, how the buildings, streets, tunnels, structures, monuments and public spaces, both open and enclosed, serve as backdrop, stage and roof for the myriad lively and life-giving activities whose totality make up the phenomenon we know as New York City.

The ultimate purpose of the guide is to enable New Yorkers— permanent or temporary— to enjoy themselves while at home and abroad in the city. It attempts to tie landmarks, whether world-renowned or obscure, to their models and their architectural and historical relatives.

Norval White and Elliot Wilensky have produced the best of the AIA initiated guides. It is a compendium of data and small photographs of buildings, places and things aimed at the professional.

AIA Guide to New York City
Norval White, Elliot Wilensky, Editors
1968
464 pp
5" x 10 1/4"
$6.95
Macmillan Co.
866 Third Avenue
New York, New York 10022

copyright by New York Chapter
American Institute of Architects

Pages from Nicholson shown actual size

Slough Hospital
Bucks. Powell & Moya 1966. A widespread hospital with interesting ward blocks and administrative tower.

South Bank Arts Centre * — M 23
Between Waterloo and Hungerford bridges SE1. G.L.C., 1965. Has now reached the second major stage in its redevelopment. These new buildings form an uncompromising and sculptural group in rough boarded concrete which should add considerably to the scope of cultural activities in London.

The Royal Festival Hall — M 23
Junction of Waterloo Rd & Belvedere Rd SE1. L.C.C., Robert Matthew and Leslie Martin, 1951. Has now been altered with improved facilities, and linked by generous pedestrian walkways to the new:

Queen Elizabeth Hall * a small concert hall seating 1,100 with a recital room and exhibition gallery.

The National Film Theatre — M 24
South Bank SE1. L.C.C., 1952. Also forms part of the Arts Centre. Sited under Waterloo Bridge.

U.S.A. Embassy — F 17
Grosvenor Square W1. Eero Saarinen with Yorke Rosenberg & Mardall, 1958–61. A serious and sensitive attempt to relate to the scale and feeling of the remaining three sides of Grosvenor Square.

Schools & colleges

Bousfield Primary School
Old Brompton Rd SW7. Chamberlin, Powell and Bon, 1955. An imaginative and cheerful environment with an open-air auditorium-classroom.

Catford County School
Bellingham Rd SE6. L.C.C., 1954. Built on a podium on the ridge of a hill, with a 4-storey classroom block linked to the assembly hall block.

Chelsea College of Science & Technology & Chelsea School of Art — L 8
Kings Rd–Manresa Rd SW3. L.C.C., 1962–4. Includes a 100ft high hostel block for 184 students; a communal block with dining rooms, assembly hall and rooms for student activities; a College extension; the new Chelsea School of Art and a new Fire Station.

Imperial College of Science & Technology — G 10
Prince Consort Rd SW7. Various new buildings, including the:
Biochemistry Building by the Architects Co-Partnership.
Halls of Residence — G 11
Princes Gardens SW7. Richard Sheppard, Robson & Partners, 1963. A cleverly planned and strongly modelled building housing over 400 students. See also:
Weekes' Hall across the Gardens by the same Architects.

Mayfield Comprehensive School
92 West Hill SW15. Powell & Moya, 1955. One of the best post-war schools in London. An existing school of 800 expanded into a comprehensive school of over 2,000 without loss of scale. Note the good gymnasia and assembly hall.

Royal College of Art * — F 10
Kensington Gore SW7. H. T. Cadbury-Brown, Sir Hugh Casson & R. Y. Goodden, 1962–64. A new college with a strong personality. An 8-storey teaching block facing Hyde Park. Good interiors, particularly the foyers and the Gulbenkian Hall.

St Paul's Choir School * — M 29
St Paul's Churchyard, EC4. Architects Co-Partnership 1967. A sensitive and deliberately scaled down design in Portland stone with a lead covered top storey in the shadow of the Cathedral.

Universities

Some of the most exciting post-war work has been within existing Universities, and in the design and construction of the new Universities.

Cambridge University. See the excellent publication, 'Cambridge New Architecture' 7s6d from Trinity Hall, Cambridge.
St John's College * new rooms, Powell & Moya 1967.
Gonville and Cains * Harvey Court, Sir Leslie Martin and Colin St J. Wilson.
Churchill College. Richard Sheppard, Robson and Partners 1961–65, (new college and winner of a limited competition).
New Hall (new women's college) Chamberlain Powell and Bon 1964–67.
Fitzwilliam House (new college) Denys Lasdun and Partners 1961–67.
Corpus Christi College * Leckhampton House, Philip Dowson 1963.
History Faculty and Library, Sidgwick Avenue, James Stirling 1967.

Essex University * One of the new Universities, near Colchester, designed by the Architects Co-Partnership, with the first buildings in use since 1965, including fine brick tower halls of residence.

Oxford University
St Catherines College * (a new college) Prof Arne Jacobsen.
Brasenose College, new rooms, Powell & Moya.
Law Library complex, Sir Leslie Martin and Colin St J. Wilson 1962.
St John * College new rooms. Architects Co-Partnership 1960.
St Anne's College. Howell Killick Partridge & Amis 1964.

Sussex University *
An interesting new University between Brighton and Lewes, planned on a handsome campus in monumental brick and vaulted concrete by Basil Spence, in association with Gordon Collins. The first stage was completed in 1962–63.

The 'new towns'

The 20th century 'new towns' were generated by the concept of the 'garden city' by Ebenezer Howard, as a counter to the big city, to provide self-contained industrial towns limited in extent by a country belt. The first of these was:

Letchworth, Herts, commenced in 1904 to the plans of Raymond Unwin.

Welwyn Garden City
followed, with the purchase of the site in 1919 with £5,000 of borrowed money. Planned in broad avenues by Louis de Soissons, this reached a population of 13,500 in 1938, increased to 50,000 in 1948.

Basildon, Essex
Near the Southend Road for 106,000 population. Has been planned very much with the motor-car in mind, with a conscious attempt to segregate pedestrians in residential areas.

Bracknell, Berks
3 miles S.W. of Maidenhead, raised from a population of 25,000 to 54,000 in 1961, and planned with four neighbourhoods. Point Royal tower block of flats by Philip Dowson is notable.

Crawley, Surrey
30 miles from London on the Brighton Road, for a population of 50,000 in 9 neighbourhood centres. A compact town centre, architecturally undistinguished.

Harlow, Essex *
Frederick Gibberd (in 1947) 80,000 population. The most interesting of the 'new towns'. Preserves large areas of existing landscape to separate the compact residential groupings. Interesting flats and patio houses at Bishopfield and Charters Cross by Michael Neylan, Old Orchard by Clifford Culpin and Partners, fine town centre, and railway station.

Hatfield, Herts
Town of 25,000 designed by Lionel Brett, and related to the nearby Hemel Hempstead. Excellent single-storey terrace houses with internal courts at the Ryde, by George Perkin.

Hemel Hempstead, Herts
Designed around the existing town, by G. A. Jellicoe in 1947, a plan not approved until 1952, as it was found to be a much more difficult process to graft a new town onto an existing community than to start on a virgin site. Town Hall complex by Clifford Culpin & Partners, (1966).

Stevenage, Herts
30 miles from London on the Great North Road, for a population of 60,000, and featuring one of the most successful traffic-free shopping centres.

Museums and parks

Museums & Galleries

London's national museums and galleries contain some of the richest treasures in the world. Admission is free and access to special items or collections not on show is willingly and trustfully given. In addition, the national museums offer a free service of advice and scholarly reference unequalled anywhere in the world. Note that their reference libraries and print collections are further described under 'Reference Libraries'.

The British Museum, the V & A and other national galleries give expert opinion on the age or identity of objects or paintings – they will not however give you a valuation.

Apart from the museums owned by the nation, London is further enriched by other collections open to the public. Most were started as specialist collections of wealthy men or associations but are now available to all, by right or courtesy. They are continually being improved and extended and are an invaluable part of our culture and history.

Artillery Museum
The Rotunda, Woolwich Common SE18. (01) 854 2424. The Rotunda was an architectural 'tent' once erected in St James's Park (1814). Little known collection of guns and muskets. *Open 10.00–12.45 & 14.00–17.00 or dusk (Sun 14.00–17.00 or dusk)*

Arts Council Gallery — M 23
Hayward Gallery, Belvedere Rd (South Bank) SE1. (01) 928 3144. Now moved from St James's Square. Temporary exhibitions of current interest – anything from James Gilray to Matisse.

Bethnal Green Museum
Cambridge Heath Rd E2. (01) 980 2415. English domestic art 18 & 19th cent. Spitalfields silks and original designs. Dolls, toys, dolls' houses and model theatres. *Open 10.00–18.00 (Sun 14.30–18.00) Closed G Fri Xmas* Free.

British Museum * — G 24
Gt. Russell St WC1. (01) 636 1555. One of the largest and greatest museums in the world. Contains famous collections of Egyptian, Assyrian, Greek and Roman, British, Oriental and Asian antiquities. Among many outstanding and unique items are the Egyptian mummies; the colossal Assyrian bulls and lions in the Nimrud gallery; the Benin, Cambodian and Chinese collections, the Elgin Marbles and the Rosetta Stone. Building 1823–47 by Sir Robert Smirke; the domed reading room 1857 is by Sidney Smirke. *Open 10.00–17.00 (Sun 14.30–18.00) Closed Xmas G Fri* Free. Lecture tours.

British Theatre Museum — D 4
Leighton House, 12 Holland Park Rd W14. (01) 937 3052. British theatre from 18th cent to present day. Special collections of Henry Irving, Pauline Chase, English Stage Company archives and the Debenham photo collection. *Open 11.00–17.00 Closed Sun, Mon, Wed Fri, B Hol* Free.

British Transport Museum
Clapham High St SW4. (01) 622 3241. Large and exciting collections on the history and development of public transport. Royal railway coaches, locomotives, vintage trains and buses. Early posters and other graphic work. *Open 10.00–17.30 Closed Sun G Fri Xmas Box* 2s6d.

Chartered Insurance Institute's Museum — M 30
20 Aldermanbury EC2. (01) 606 3835. Collection of Insurance Companies' fire marks. Fire fighting equipment, helmets, etc. *Open 09.15–17.15 Closed Sat & Sun* Free.

Commonwealth Institute — D 6
230 Kensington High St W8. (01) 937 8252. Scenery, natural resources, way of life and industrial development of Commonwealth countries. Reference library of current Commonwealth literature. Cinema, art exhibitions. *Open 10.00–17.30 (Sun 14.30–18.00) Closed G Fri Xmas* Free

Courtauld Institute Galleries — F 24
Woburn Square WC1. (01) 580 1015. The Courtauld Collection of French Impressionists (including fine paintings by Cezanne, Van Gogh, Gaugin) and the Lee, Gambier-Parry and Fry Collections. *Open 10.00–17.00 (Sun 14.00–17.00). Closed G Fri X Eve Xmas* Free.

The Cuming Museum
Walworth Rd SE17. (01) 703 3324. Southwark's Roman and Medieval local history. The Lovett collection of London superstitions. *Open 10.00–17.30 (Thur 19.00, Sat 17.00) Closed Sun* Free.

Dulwich College Picture Gallery *
College Rd SE21. (01) 693 5254. English, Italian, Dutch and French paintings exhibited in one of the most beautiful art galleries in England. Notable works by Rembrandt, Rubens and Gainsborough. Building by Sir John Soane 1811–14. *Open May–Aug 10.00–18.00 (Sun from 14.00) Sep–Apr 10.00–16.00 (Sun from 14.00) Closed Mon*

Embroiders Guild — E 19
73 Wimpole St W1. (01) 935 3281. Unusual collection in a private house. Library and museum of historical specimens. Advisory body.

Fenton House
Hampstead Grove NW3. (01) 435 3471. The Benton-Fletcher collection of early keyboard instruments and the Binning collection of porcelain and furniture. *Open 10.00–13.00 & 14.00–17.00 (Sun 14.00–17.00 or dusk) Closed Tue Xmas Box* 2s6d.

Foundling Hospital — F 26
40 Brunswick Square WC1. (01) 278 1911. Small gallery of 18th cent English painters, including Hogarth, Gainsborough and Kneller. Founded by Hogarth. *Open Mon & Fri 10.00–12.00 & 14.00–16.00 Closed G Fri B Hol X Eve Xmas Box* Free.

Geffrye Museum
Kingsland Rd E2. (01) 739 8368. 18th cent almshouses. Period rooms and furniture from 1600 to the present day. *Open 10.00–17.00 (Sun 14.00–17.00) Closed Mon G Fri B Hol Xmas* Free.

Geological Museum * — H 9
Exhibition Rd SW7. (01) 589 9441. Physical and economic geology and mineralogy of the world; regional geology of Britain. Models, dioramas and a large collection of gems, stones and fossils. *Open 10.00–18.00 (Sun 14.30–18.00) Closed G Fri Xmas* Free.

Goldsmiths' Hall — L 29
Foster Lane WC2. (01) 606 8971. Fine collection of antique plate. The largest collection of modern silver and jewellery in the country. *By appointment*

Gordon Medical Museum — Q 29
St Thomas' St SE1 (01) 407 7600. Collection of specimens and models dealing with diseases in humans. *By application to Dean of Medical School or curator*

Guildhall Museum — M 30
Bassishaw High Walk, off Basinghall St EC2. (01) 606 3030 Ext 417. History and archaeology of London. Collections of Saxon, Roman and Medieval finds from the City. *Open 10.00–17.00 Closed Sun G Fri B Hol Xmas* Free.

Hampton Court Palace
Hampton Court, Middx. (01) 977 2141. Individual collection of Italian masterpieces. Giorgione, Titan, Tintoretto and early primitives. Also wall and ceiling paintings by Thornhill, Vanbrugh and Verrio. *For times see under 'Historic London'*

Horniman Museum
100 London Rd SE23. (01) 699 2339. Natural history, ethnography, musical instruments. The building (1901) by C. Harrison Townsend is 'Art Nouveau'. Aquarium and reference library. *Open 10.30–18.00 (Sun 14.00–18.00) Closed X Eve Xmas* Free.

Imperial War Museum

Natural History Museum

Imperial War Museum * — Q 23
Lambeth Rd SE1. (01) 735 8922. Very popular national museum of all aspects of war since 1914. Collection of models, weapons, paintings, relics. The building was once a lunatic asylum. *Open 10.00–18.00 (Sun 14.00–18.00) Closed G Fri Xmas* Free.

The Iveagh Bequest, Kenwood *
Hampstead Lane NW3. (01) 348 1286. Fine house by Robert Adam. Paintings by Rembrandt, Vermeer, Reynolds and Gainsborough. *Open 10.00–19.00 Winter 18.00 or dusk (Sun 14.00–19.00 Winter 18.00 or dusk) Closed G Fri X Eve Xmas* Free.

Jewish Museum — E 25
Woburn House, Upper Woburn Place WC1. (01) 387 3081. A comprehensive collection of ritual objects and other antiquities illustrating Jewish life and worship. *Open Mon–Thur 14.30–17.00 (Fri & Sun 10.30–12.45) Closed Sat B Hol & Jewish Holy Days* Free.

Leathercraft Museum — M 30
Gillett House, 55 Basinghall St EC2. (01) 606 3030 Ext 417. The use of leather by the London guilds. *Open 10.00–17.00 Closed Sun G Fri B Hol, Xmas* Free.

Leighton House — D 4
12 Holland Park Rd W14. (01) 937 9916. British 19th cent artists; Leighton, Burne-Jones, Watts. Arab hall with decorations of 14–16th cent Oriental tiles. *Open 11.00–17.00 Closed G Fri X Eve Xmas Box B Hol* Free.

London Museum * — D 9
Kensington Palace, Kensington Gardens W8. (01) 937 9816. Previously a Royal residence designed by Wren and Kent. The life and history of London from Roman times to

present day. Antiquities, costume, pictures, coronation robes, the London theatre, toys and games, fire engines. Also 'Orangery' and gardens. *Open 10.00–18.00, Winter 17.00 (Sun 14.00–18.00, Winter 17.00) Closed G Fri X Eve Xmas Box* Free.

M.C.C. Memorial Gallery
Lord's Cricket Ground NW8. (01) 289 1611. The history of cricket. *Open Mon–Fri 09.30–16.30 (Matchdays 10.30 until close of play)* 1s.

Madame Tussaud's * — B 19
Baker Street Station NW1. (01) 935 3726. Waxwork effigies of the famous and notorious. Battle of Trafalgar and 'Heroes live'. *Open 10.00–17.30 (18.30 Sat & Sun)* 7s 6d. Joint ticket with Planetarium 10s.

Martinware Pottery Collection
Public Library, 9–11 Osterley Park Rd, Southall, Middx. (01) 574 3412. Collection of Martinware, including birds, face mugs and grotesques. *Open 09.00–20.00 (Sat 09.00–17.00) Closed Sun* Free.

National Gallery * — J 21
Trafalgar Square WC2. (01) 930 7618. Very fine repre-

Nicholson's London Guide is one of the most convenient and comprehensive pocket guides to any major metropolitan center in the world.

"Twelve pages of street maps; complete street index; easy color location reference; river map; all parking places; enormous shopping guide; complete sports guide; Cry for Help' and 'Emergency' sections; London for the down-and-out or the desperate. Also the only complete lavatory guide in existence."

Shown here, in actual size, are several pages from this most remarkable pocket guide. The maps are color cross indexed with the listings and the information included, as you can see by the table of contents, is particularly useful to the visitor. I envy their ability to put so much so clearly in such a small space.

Introduction

Over the past year, I and a team of experts, have been working on this new edition of the guide to extend its scope without losing its original pocket size and fine quality printing.

Our aim has been to help Londoners and tourists both to enjoy London and to deal with any emergency. It is apparent that this book is providing an essential public service. Realising this we have given special attention to this factor throughout. For instance the 'Cry for Help' section is now more detailed and comprehensive, 'Childrens London' has added chapters for the ever increasing interest of children and parents in cultural and educational activities – such as 'Bird-watching', 'Trips out of London', 'Zoos, aquaria and aviaries'. For students there is an entirely new section dealing with their requirements, such as holidays, clubs, and accommodation.

In addition to the red star ✳ for outstanding distinction I have provided for the needs of people on a limited budget by introducing a quick reference blue spot ● indicating good value for money. The shopping guide is considerably enlarged, more comprehensive and authoritative. There is a new easy-to-read bus map and the special inclusion of a night bus map in the 'All-night London' section.

No advertising is carried. No one can buy a place in the guide. Every entry is here on its own merit.

I hope this guide will give help and pleasure and fulfil its aims. I would welcome any suggestions that might add to its value.

Robert Nicholson

Contents

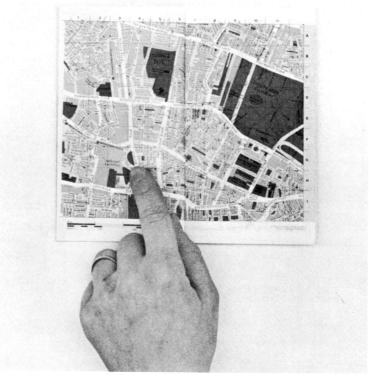

Nicholson's London Guide
Robert Nicholson Publications
1968
128 pp
3 3/4" x 6 3/4"
7/6 ($.90)
Seymour Press
334 Brixton Road
London SW1, England

Michelin's Green Guides

From the Empire State Building to Grand Army Plaza (59th Street)

EMPIRE STATE BUILDING ★★★

However you arrive in New York, by land, sea or air, the Empire State Building stands out as a landmark, its tower rising above Manhattan, shining at a height of 1472 feet. Named for New York the Empire State, its 102 stories make it the tallest building in the world.

The view from the top is so splendid that it deserves two visits : first by daylight, to understand the layout of New York; and then again in the evening, to enjoy the spectacle of the city's lights.

The construction. — Less than two years after the first excavations in October 1929, the building was opened in May 1931. Work progressed at a dizzy pace; at times, more than a floor rose each day. There are only two stories of foundations, but 60,000 tons of steel beams (enough for a double-track railroad from New York to Baltimore) also support the tower. These were in place within three days of their production in Pittsburgh. The whole building weighs 365,000 tons, less than the weight of the 55 feet of dirt and rock excavated to build it.

At first the public was very apprehensive about the stability of the building but it seems to have proved durable. Seventy-four elevators serve the 102 floors, and 5 acres of windows are washed twice a month. It takes half an hour to walk down the 1860 steps. During the 1945 elevator strike, these steps were well used. One waiter brought coffee and 150 sandwiches to workers marooned on the 31st floor, and was rewarded for his efforts by a tip of $75.

Empire State and Eiffel Tower.

"The Michelin maps and guides are edited and designed in a turn-of-the-century, white glazed-tile building on one of the outer boulevards of Paris. The scrupulous respect for information, the constant revision and the high communicative value of their design are the result of the team-work of 200 specialists, including seventy cartographers. The three main publications are the maps, the green-cover French tourist guides, and the red-cover Michelin guides to hotels and restaurants. Concern for reliability is matched by an extremely clear editorial structure providing:

(a) Basic data on 3700 towns and villages, their attractions, distances from other towns, timetables of ferries, custom houses, etc.

(b) Town maps with cross routes, main places of interest, monuments, hotels, restaurants, main garages, one-way streets, restricted parking zones, etc.

(c) A selected list of garages, their specialization or affiliation, their working hours for Sundays and night service.

(d) An extensive, graded selection of hotels and restaurants of all classes with indication of up-to-date prices and comforts.

This information is tabulated clearly, with typographic common sense, and notes in four languages."

"Before 1923 all lettering on maps was in black. Then, as some regions became overloaded with data it became necessary to lighten the information of lesser importance by printing it in a light colour. The basic colour system is at present red for main road networks, yellow for secondary roads, and white for the others.

From the Empire State Building to Grand Army Plaza (59th Street)

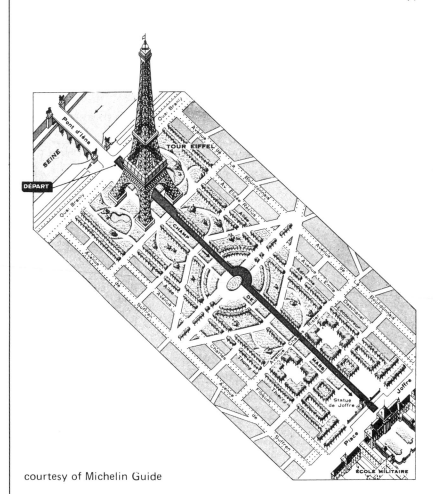

FIFTH AVENUE
FROM THE
EMPIRE STATE BUILDING
TO GRAND ARMY PLAZA

courtesy of Michelin Guide

The 222-foot television antenna was added in 1951. It is a mere 22 stories high. In 1960 the beacon light was installed. It can be seen from 100 miles away, and is so powerful that it is turned off during the spring and fall migratory bird seasons. Otherwise, the birds would be blinded, and would fly directly into the building by the thousands. The Empire State cost almost $40,000,000 to build. Fifteen thousand people work there, and 35,000 visit it daily. A battery of 200 cleaning women wield the vacuum cleaner on off hours. The building belongs to the Crown family of Chicago.

Visit. — Before going inside, walk a few yards along East 34th or 33rd Street, to obtain the dizzy effect of perspective.

Ascent to the Observatory★★★. — *Enter the ticket office from 34th Street. The Observatory is open from 9:30 AM to midnight (admission : $1.50). Consult the visibility notice before buying your tickets.*

You may have to stand in line : an average of 35,000 people visit every day. The express elevator will take you to the 80th floor in less than a minute. The cabin is pressurized, but you will want to swallow or yawn to avoid popping or buzzing in your ears. Take a second elevator to the 80th floor Observatory (cafeteria, souvenir stands).

Here a rectangular open platform permits you to enjoy a magnificent **panoramic view★★★** for 50 miles in each direction when it is clear.

You may shudder to think that one July day in 1945, a bomber crashed into the building, at the level of the 78th and 79th floors.

On bad days, or when the crowd is not too large, we advise you to take another elevator to the circular upper observatory which is glass enclosed.

Panoramic routes are green. Rivers, lakes, canals, and the sea are of course blue. Representation of relief, given up in 1923, is being remodeled for a new issue of maps."

"The yearly collection of information for the continuous process of rejuvenation flows to both maps and guides, as the value of each is determined by how up to date they are. The Michelin services digest 50,000 survey documents a year, compare them with descriptive tape recordings taken on site, and interview public works officials to feed their cartography department with tabulations of changes that have occurred."

New York City
Michelin
1968
144 pp
4 3/4" x 10"
$3.50
French and European Publications
610 Fifth Avenue
New York, New York 10020

**Rettig's
Ten walking tours
of Cambridge**

Covering essentially the whole city of Cambridge, Massachusetts, in a series of ten neighborhood tours, this book describes hundreds of buildings of all sorts—institutional, commercial, residential. Each building is illustrated with a small photograph; the date of construction and the name of the architect, when known, are given, together with a succinct comment by the author.

This is the most rigorously produced walking tour guide of a city I know of. Unfortunately, the photographs show the buildings as individual jewels in the landscape as opposed to the way you would see them as you walk by.

Guide to Cambridge Architecture
Ten Walking Tours
Robert Bell Rettig
1969
224 pp
8'' x 5''
$3.95
The M.I.T. Press
50 Ames Street
Cambridge, Massachusetts 02142

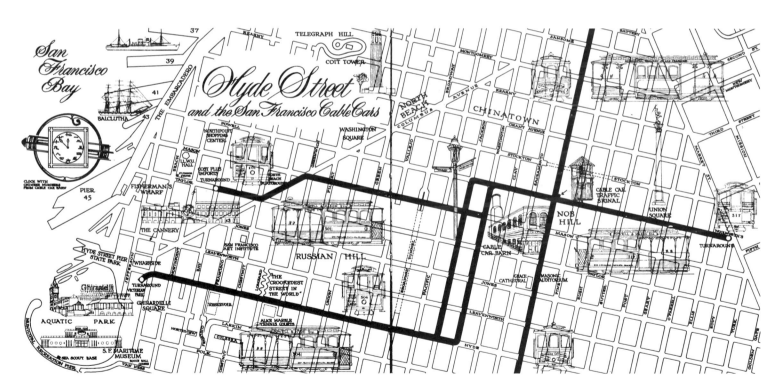

This publication includes walking and driving tours of those attractions in San Francisco and the bay area presumed to be of the greatest interest to children. Maps isolate and identify significant structures.

This book turns out to be drives for adults with children in their cars in San Francisco. Nevertheless the maps, although not particularly to my taste, are useful and the idea of doing a book for children is to be commended.

**Walks for Children in
San Francisco**
Margot Patterson Doss
Maps by Len Darwin
1970
64 pp
8'' x 8''
$2.95
Grove Press Inc.
53 East 11th Street
New York, New York 10003

Each tour includes an hour of actual cassette tape time, equivalent to four to seven hours of tour time, depending on the pace the traveler sets for himself. Six different cassettes are now available — walking tours of Amsterdam, London, Paris and Rome, and driving tours of the English and French countrysides. Each tape comes complete with a detailed map of the tour area.

Pan Am Tours on tape offer travelers several bonus conveniences:
1) travelers can familiarize themselves with a tour before leaving the hotel room
2) they can see and hear simultaneously, thus eliminating the nuisance of continually glancing at a guidebook
3) the narrative includes precise instructions on getting from one spot on the tour to the next
4) the tapes provide a permanent narrative of the tour and can be used to accompany slides and film
5) a blank cassette is provided with each Pan Am recorder for those who wish to record their own impressions.

The idea is terrific, the execution only average. I would hope that further generations of this idea either by Pan American or others improve the quality of their map and soundtrack.

Pan American Taped Tours
London, Paris, Rome, Amsterdam, English Countryside, Fontainbleau and Versailles
$2.95 cassette
$19.95 tape player with tape
Pan American World Airways
(or your travel agent)
Box 5337
Detroit, Michigan 48211

Appleyard, Lynch
and Myer's
View from the Road

44

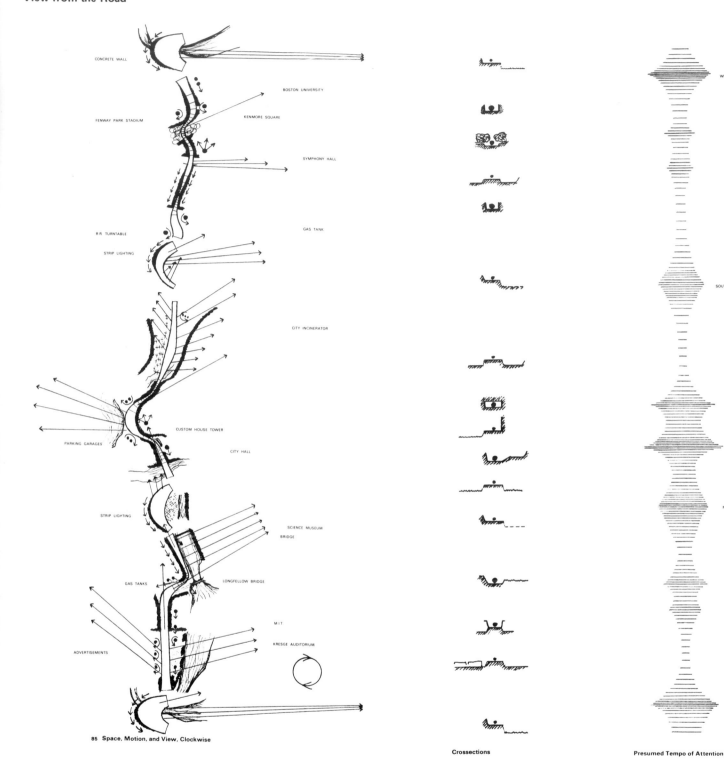

CONCRETE WALL

BOSTON UNIVERSITY

FENWAY PARK STADIUM

KENMORE SQUARE

SYMPHONY HALL

R R TURNTABLE

GAS TANK

STRIP LIGHTING

CITY INCINERATOR

CUSTOM HOUSE TOWER

PARKING GARAGES

CITY HALL

STRIP LIGHTING

SCIENCE MUSEUM

BRIDGE

GAS TANKS

LONGFELLOW BRIDGE

M I T

KRESGE AUDITORIUM

ADVERTISEMENTS

85 Space, Motion, and View, Clockwise

Crossections

WEST INTERSECTION

SOUTH INTERSECTION

NORTH INTERSECTION

WEST INTERSECTION

Presumed Tempo of Attention

"This monograph deals with the esthetics of highways: the way they look to the driver and his passengers, and what this implies for their design. We emphasize the potential beauty of these great engineering achievements, as contrasted with their current ugliness. Since the realization of this visual potential lies in the hands of the men who design them, this monograph is addressed to the highway engineer. We hope that he will find our ideas of use."

"We became interested in the esthetics of highways out of a concern with the visual formlessness of our cities and an intuition that the new expressway might be one of our best means of reestablishing coherence and order on the new metropolitan scale. We were also attracted to the highway because it is a good example of a design issue typical of the city: the problem of designing visual sequences for the observer in motion. But if in the end the study contributes something toward making the highway experience a more enjoyable one, we will be well satisfied."

"Most of our particular conclusions are the result of a series of studies of existing highways and of people's reactions to them. They have been further modified by our attempt to develop appropriate methods of design. Chapter 1 contains a summary of our findings and conjectures, while Chapter 2 proposes a new graphic language for describing visual sequences on the highway. Chapters 3 and 4 use these concepts and this language to analyze the impact of an existing road, and to illustrate how a new road might be designed."

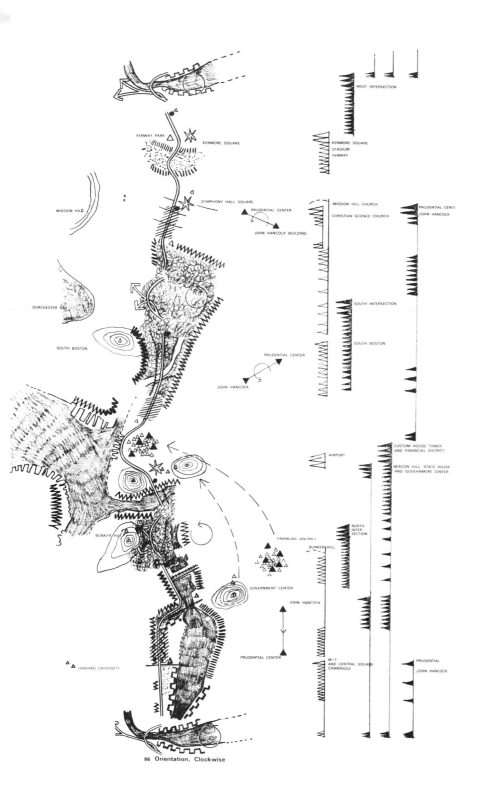

86 Orientation, Clockwise

*Sequence experience notation
first came to my attention in an
article by the same name by
Philip Thiel in the Town Planning
Review of April 1961. The View
from the Road is an enriching
outgrowth of that idea (which
is not to say that Thiel's piece
was its source). Appleyard,
Lynch and Myer have produced
a veritable dictionary· of sequence
space notation. Especially useful to the student, the para-pro-
fessional and the professional.*

View from the Road
Donald Appleyard, Kevin Lynch
and John R. Myer
1964
64 pp
9 1/2'' x 15 1/8''
$15.00
The M.I.T. Press
50 Ames Street
Cambridge, Massachusetts 02142

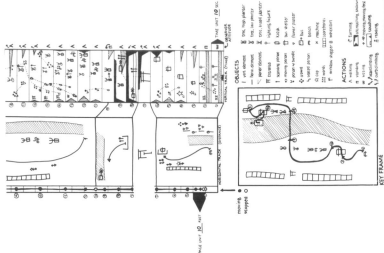

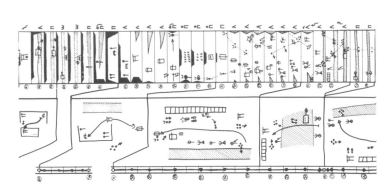

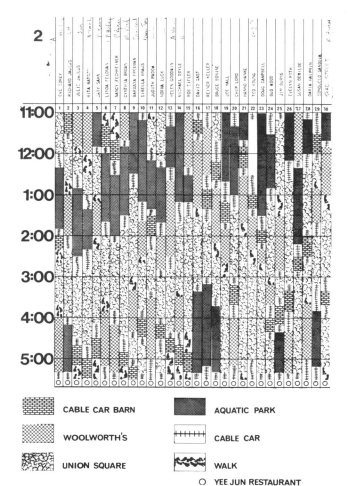

		CABLE CAR BARN				AQUATIC PARK
WOOLWORTH'S					CABLE CAR	
UNION SQUARE					WALK	
		○	YEE JUN RESTAURANT			

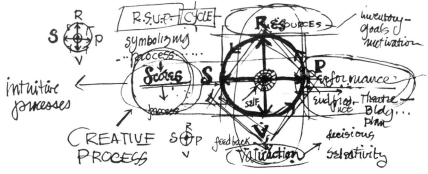

"This book started as an explanation of 'scores' and the interrelationships between scoring in the various fields of art. Scores are symbolizations of processes which extend over time."

"I saw scores as a way of describing all such processes in all of the arts, of making process visible and thereby designing with process through scores."

"I hope that scores will lead into new ways of designing and planning large-scale environments of regions and large communities whose essential nature is complexity and whose purpose is diversity."

". . . the second half of the book describes street scores, ecological scoring, city scores, and finally community scores."

Mr. Halprin continues to develop his innovative movement notation systems and this new book profusely describes what he calls "scores." There is a feeling of Klee about some of the drawings.

As in the case of Image of the City shown on the following page, I wonder about its general language applicability.

RSVP Cycles
Lawrence Halprin
1969
207 pp
9" x 9"
$15.00
George Braziller, Inc.
One Park Avenue
New York, New York 10016

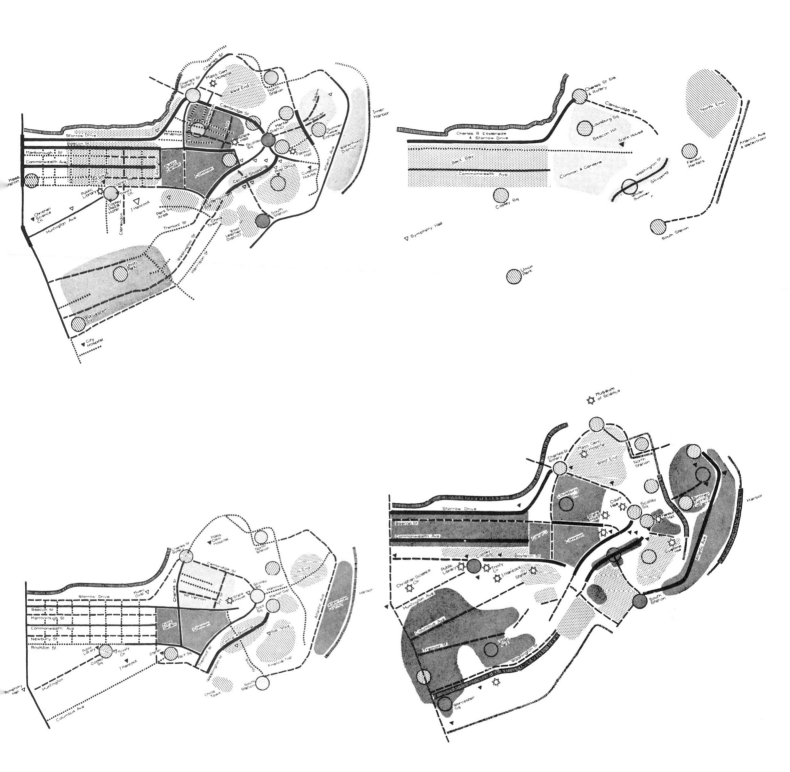

"This book is about the look of cities, and whether this look is of any importance, and whether it can be changed. The urban landscape, among its many roles is also something to be seen, to be remembered, and to delight in. Giving visual form to the city is a special kind of design problem, and a rather new one at that."

"In the course of examining this new problem, the book looks at three American cities: Boston, Jersey City and Los Angeles."

Mr. Lynch formulates a new criterion — imageability — and shows its potential value as a guide for the building and rebuilding of cities.

It would be interesting to develop a notation system similar to the one used here, but more rigorous in its display, that would enable one to combine it with statistics that might have been gathered by a more mechanical means. In the hands of Kevin Lynch this book represents an excellent tool. I'm concerned with its general use by those with less facility.

Image of the City
Kevin Lynch
1960
194 pp
5 1/4" x 8"
$2.95
The M.I.T. Press
50 Ames Street
Cambridge, Massachusetts 02142

ZÜRICH

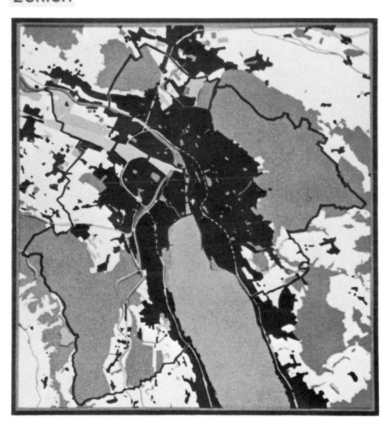

BERN

Der ausgedehnte öffentliche Bodenbesitz, zirka 53,8 % des gesamten Stadtgebietes, liegt in den Händen von Bund, Staat, Einwohnergemeinde und Burgergemeinde. Der Hauptanteil fällt auf die Burgergemeinde, in deren Besitz sich die schönen Waldungen um die Stadt befinden. Durch Ausscheidungsvertrag vom Jahre 1852 zwischen Burgergemeinde und Einwohnergemeinde ist die Einwohnergemeinde zu einem ansehnlichen Grundbesitz gekommen. Dieser ist besonders im letzten Dezennium systematisch durch Ankauf vergrössert worden und ist das Ergebnis einer zielbewussten Bodenpolitik. Der private Bodenbesitz ist mehr in Kleinparzellen aufgeteilt. Weder in privaten Händen noch in der Hand von Terraingesellschaften befinden sich grössere, zusammenhängende Komplexe.

Gelb: Öffentlicher Besitz; weiss: Privater Besitz

ZÜRICH

Vom Grundeigentum der Stadt Zürich sind 711,11 ha Wald und ca. 68,80 ha Allmend; vom privaten Grundbesitz sind ca. 581 ha Wald und ca. 4 ha. private Strassenfläche. Das städtische Grundeigentum wird systematisch durch Zukauf vermehrt. Die Abgabe von realisierbaren städtischen Liegenschaften erfolgt grösstenteils an Genossenschaften mit gemeinnützigem Charakter. Der Privatbesitz ist im wesentlichen in Kleinparzellen aufgekauft. Die Bebauung der Splitterparzellen erfolgt in den letzten Jahren zum überwiegenden Teil durch private und gemeinnützige Genossenschaften. Ausserhalb der Stadtgrenzen hat die Stadt Zürich ca. 1142 ha Grundeigentum, zum grössten Teil aus Wald bestehend.

Maßstab 1 : 100 000

28

A comparative study of ten Swiss cities through aerial photographs, structural elements, public and private property, traffic, street photographs, land use, green areas, population density and city growth, and statistics.

The Association of Swiss Architects (headed by Dr. Camille Martin) compiled comparable mapping material to show urban development in 10 major cities during the National Exhibition of 1911 and 1914. First displayed in an exhibition in 1928 in Zurich, Switzerland, this collection was available in book form.

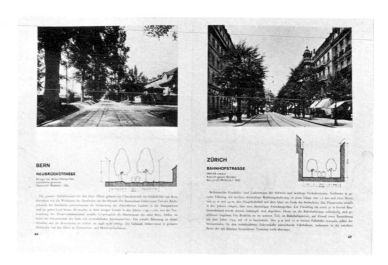

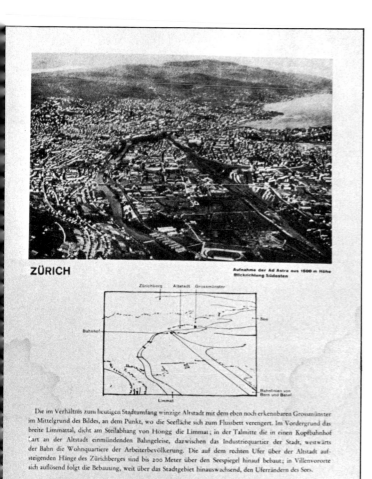

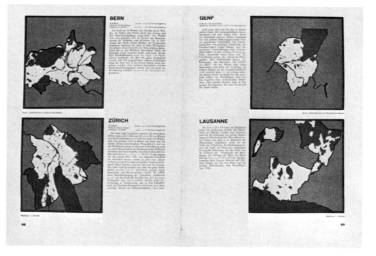

This is a rigorously conceived and executed comparative atlas of Swiss cities describing small grain information about streets and street cross sections up to aerial photography of the city and generalized regional information. It is excellent, modestly produced and unfortunately, to the best of my knowledge, unavailable.

Städtebau in der Schweiz
1929
72 pp
8 1/2'' x 11 3/4''
out of print
Wasmuth Buchhandlung und
Antiquariat
Hardenburgstrasse 9a
Berlin 12, Germany

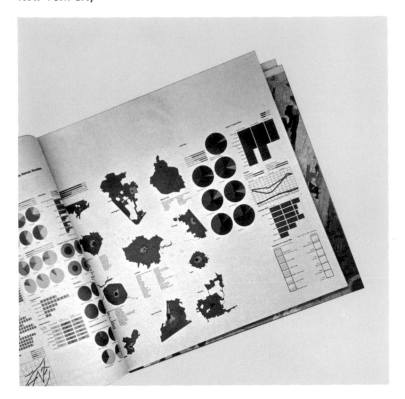

The New York City Plan consists of five volumes, one on each borough: Staten Island, Queens, Brooklyn, Bronx and Manhattan representing New York City's first comprehensive plan, and a sixth volume that is a 180 page Critical Issues Book.

"The book has 36 maps, many of them full-page. They include maps of existing and planned community facilities such as schools, colleges, hospitals,

mass transit, highways, publicly-aided housing and recreation areas; community planning, health, fire and sanitation districts, and police precincts and urban renewal areas.

"The text appraises the City today and sets forth broad goals and guidelines for the City's social and physical development focusing on four broad themes: New York as a national center of art, culture, business and finance;

the City of opportunity; the urban environment and the role of the government."

Plan for New York City
New York City Planning
Commission
1969
six volumes
17" x 17"
$15.00 each
The M.I.T. Press
50 Ames Street
Cambridge, Massachusetts 02142

Market East

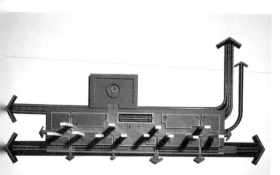

Midtown Manhattan

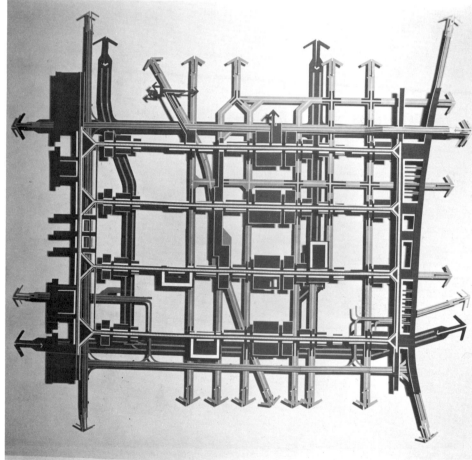

rank Williams, urban design con-ultant for Skidmore, Owings and errill, has created three dimen-onal models of enormously com-ex projects like Market Street ast (Philadelphia) and areas like idtown Manhattan which clearly emonstrate the horizontal and ertical movement systems of ach and how they mesh. Williams akes urban movement observable.

Frank Williams' models of Market East, Manhattan, and Berkeley are fine examples of the ability to communicate complex multi-level movement systems easily and beautifully. (This is one of many pages where the use of color is needed to explain the material fully.)

Frank Williams
210 Centre Street
New York, New York 10013

"The Sanborn Map Company has mapped at large scale (1'' = 50' to 1'' = 200') over 11,000 cities in the United States."

"New maps are produced using current aerial photography, together with a field inspection to add the finer details. Revision work is accomplished by field inspection."

"The conventional map sheet is approximately 22'' x 28'' and others are 11'' x 14''. An example would be the coverage of the city of Philadelphia which is contained in twenty-nine volumes, comprising 2,390 22'' x 28'' full color map sheets."

"These maps were originally designed to serve the fire insurance industry and are still used for this purpose. In the past several years the basic information has been found to be invaluable in the preparation of land use, urban renewal, noise abatement and other types of studies."

No maps in general production give more specific information about buildings, how they're made, lot lines, land use, and addresses than the Sanborn maps. A Sanborn map of the area around a school would entertain children for a whole day.

Sanborn Map Company
629 Fifth Avenue
Pelham, New York 10803

62,500

1:250,000

24,000

1:250,000

aps published by the Geological
urvey are intended to give a
cture of the terrain that is as
mplete as can be legibly
produced at the selected scale.
apping accuracy is assured by
eld surveys and photogram-
etric methods, using stereo-
opic plotting instruments
d aerial photographs.
etropolitan Area Maps, at
24,000 scale, have been pre-
red for many cities and
blished in one or more sheets,

according to the size of the area
shown.

Baltimore, Maryland is shown
here at the three major scales
employed by the Geological
Survey. Also included is
Montreal, Quebec, at 1:250,000
scale, from the Canadian Map
Distribution Office.

*The only maps done in an orderly
and complete fashion in the U.S.
are produced by the U.S. Department of the Interior. These were
used as base maps in Urban Atlas
(page 24) and are used in their
varying scales extensively.
1:24,000 is equal to one-inch is
equal to 2,000 feet.*

**U.S. Department of the Interior
Geological Survey Maps**
1:24,000
1:62,500
1:250,000
United States Geological Survey
Washington, D. C. 20242

Map Distribution Office
Department of Energy, Mines
and Resources
615 Booth Street
Ottawa 3, Canada

To get around Mexico City's new subway you don't even have to be able to read, thanks to the Metro Graphics Program of Lance Wyman. Along with other essential information, each station has a graphic symbol as part of an overall graphic design for the transportation system. Colors are keyed to help identify both the signs and the message. Each station's sign represents some historical or distinctive landmark near that station. For example, a cluster of flowers denotes Balbuena, a station located near the garden of Balbuena. The site of Salto del Aqua station was once the termination of an aquaduct and is symbolized by a fountain. Very near Mexico City's International Airport is a station whose symbol is a plane. An eagle marks Cuahtemoc station, named after an Aztec chief. Juanacatlan station, named for a "Butterfly Net," made famous by area fishermen, is marked by a butterfly symbol.

Lance Wyman's love of life which was so exuberantly displayed in his Mexican Olympics Graphics and symbology shows through in his most recent effort for the Metro in Mexico City. The pictograms used, as you can see in this double page spread, are entertaining and meaningful.

OBSERVATORIO TACUBAYA JUANACATLAN CHAPULTEPEC SEVILLA INSURGENTES CUAUHTEMOC BALDERAS SALTO DEL AGUA I LA CATOLICA PINO SUAREZ MERCED CANDELARIA SAN LAZARO MOCTEZUMA BALBUENA AEROPUERTO GOMEZ FARIAS ZARAGOZA

LINEA 1
LINEA 2
LINEA 3

Lance Wyman
118 West 80th Street
New York, New York 10024

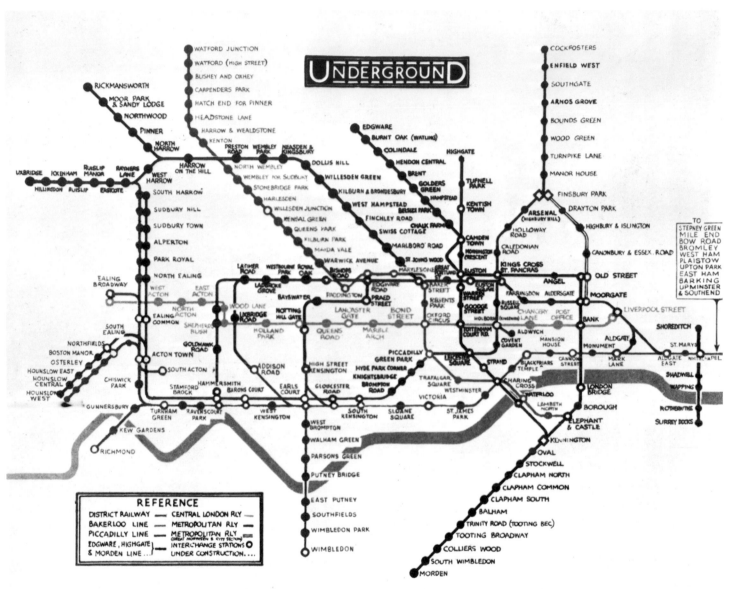

H.C.BECK 1931

The London Underground map makes a complex transportation system immediately observable without benefit of compromises requiring further explanation and detailing.

It was invented in 1932, by Harry C. Beck, a 29 year old temporary draftsman in the Establishment Office Drawing Section of the London Underground Group. There were two radical innovations which have been incorpor-

ated in all subsequent versions of the diagram, right up to the present day: (a) the enlargement of the central area of the underground system in relation to the outlying areas, so that the complicated connections at the center could be more clearly shown; (b) the limiting of the direction of route lines to verticals, horizontals, and 45° diagonals.

Every character of every word in the original version was hand-

lettered by Beck in Johnston sans-serif capitals: more than 2400 characters in all.

The L.U.G. rejected the map outright when Harry Beck submitted his first, unsolicited design in 1931. Then a limited trial number was run off for the first edition and comment was invited from the traveling public.

The Design of the London Underground Diagram
Ken Garland
pp 68—82
The Penrose Annual 1969
edited by Herbert Spencer
Hastings House
10 East 40th Street
New York, New York 10016

Pocket edition shown actual size. Original in colors.

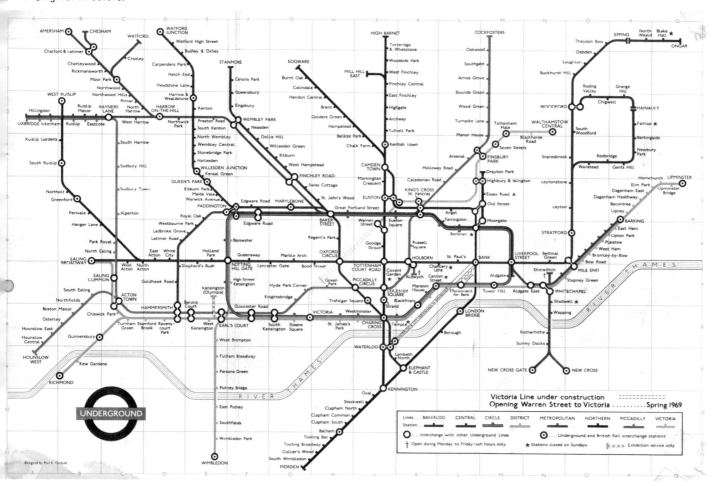

The London Underground Map is shown in its first sketch form (1931) on page 56 and in its current version on 57. This map represents a high water mark in cartographic diagrams and has fathered a whole series of derivative diagrams. Some of these have proven useful, like the new Boston map, and others like the current New York City subway map have proved disasterously unintelligible. This map has had the ability to relieve the disorientation of visitors to London over the last forty years.

London Underground Map
Harry C. Beck and
Paul E. Garbutt
40'' x 50''
7/6 ($.90)
pocket editions free
Publicity Officer
280 Old Marylebone Road
London NW1, England

Halifax bus network

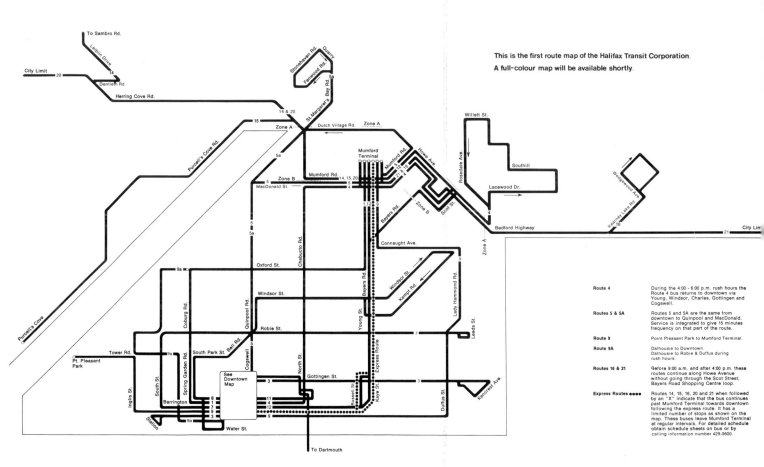

This is the first route map of the Halifax Transit Corporation.
A full-colour map will be available shortly.

Route 4	During the 4:00 - 6:00 p.m. rush hours the Route 4 bus returns to downtown via Young, Windsor, Charles, Gottingen and Cogswell.
Routes 5 & 5A	Routes 5 and 5A are the same from downtown to Quinpool and MacDonald. Service is integrated to give 15 minutes frequency on that part of the route.
Route 9	Point Pleasant Park to Mumford Terminal.
Route 9A	Dalhousie to Downtown. Dalhousie to Robie & Duffus during rush hours.
Routes 16 & 21	Before 9:00 a.m. and after 4:00 p.m. these routes continue along Howe Avenue without going through the Scot Street, Bayers Road Shopping Centre loop.
Express Routes ●●●●	Routes 14, 15, 16, 20 and 21 when followed by an "X" indicate that the bus continues past Mumford Terminal towards downtown following the express route. It has a limited number of stops as shown on the map. These buses leave Mumford Terminal at regular intervals. For detailed schedule obtain schedule sheets on bus or by calling information number 429-0600.

This graphic material represents aspects of a complete design program for Halifax transit, a bus company which operates from Halifax, Nova Scotia.

The coordinated design of the buses, street information, signs, tickets and route map, make it easy to understand and demonstrate the operation in detail and as a whole.

Gottschalk + Ash Limited
2050 Mansfield
Montreal 110, Quebec, Canada

Symbol Design: Ian Valentine
Map Design: Margrit Stutz
Client: Halifax Transit Corp.

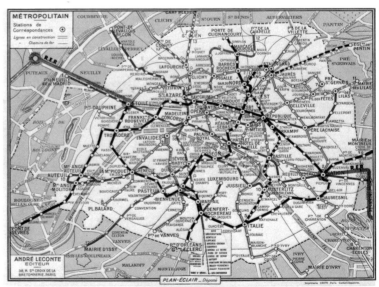

The Metro in Paris is an extra-
ordinarily complex system; it
is usual to change lines several
times in order to reach one's
destination. Many stations have
a push-button light board
which lights up the network to
be used to gain access most
efficiently to one's chosen
last stop.

Paris Metro light boards
Régie Autonome Des
Transports Parisiens
Boite Postale 70-06 Paris
53ter, Quai Des Grands-Augustins
Paris (6e) France
Michel Linon
Le Chef du Service des
Relations Exterieures

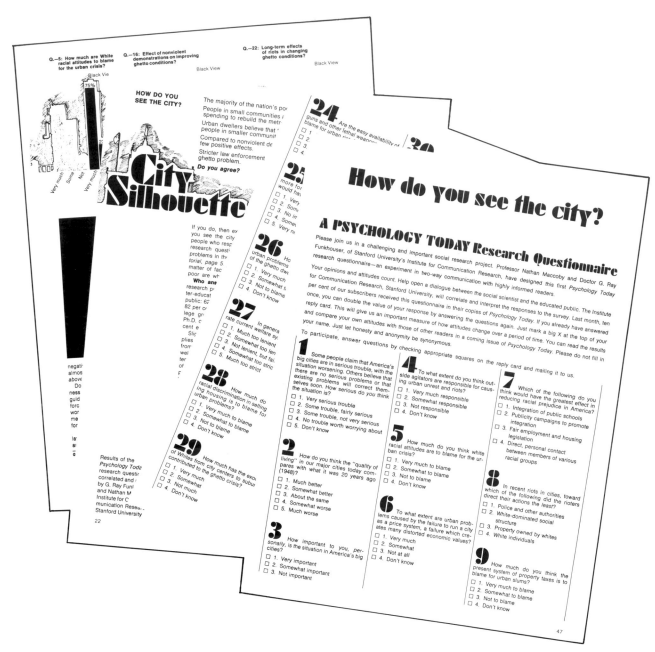

Psychology Today research questionnaires draw as many as 30,000 completed response forms. Step one is a thorough computer analysis (percentages, cross-tabulations, correlation coefficients and factor analysis). Step two is human analysis and interpretation of the computer data. The primary objective is to compress the data, to make visible and comprehensible the trends and relationships found. Graphs are made when complex relationships are best

communicated visually. Color is used, when available, to clarify relationships or separate compound data and for decorative purposes. The test and tables are intermingled in the copy, each supporting and leading into the other so that the reader can go through the report smoothly, without having to flip from one page to the other looking for data.

Part of urban communication is urban responsibility. The ability to articulate a good question in order to elicit valued response and then display these tabulations in a form understandable to a general public (or in this case to a large readership) is done at a consistently high level by Psychology Today, a magazine whose informative art direction and interest in urban information is worthy of note.

Psychology Today
August 1968 and
December 1968
8 1/2'' x 11''
subscription: $7.00 per year
P.O. Box 60461
Terminal Annex
Los Angeles, California 90060

"The aim of this book is to make the graphic designer more aware of diagrams, their use and design."

"The book has three parts, each covering different aspects of the subject: statistical diagrams, explanatory and statistical maps, explanatory diagrams. There is a final section which briefly discusses problems of technique and includes notes on books that deal in more detail with certain aspects of the subject."

"The various ways of showing statistics or providing explanatory drawings by diagram or on map are described. The best uses for and the disadvantages of each method are discussed. The text is fully supported by the illustrations and their captions. There is as wide a selection as possible with examples from many countries: the United States, Germany, France, Sweden, Japan and other countries. Diagram methods

are part of the language of international communication. The diagrams come from a wide variety of sources: atlas, encyclopedia, school and university text book, scientific magazine, newspaper, advertisement, and television."

"The illustrations in this book are important. The designer will see more quickly from example than from description the effectiveness of using a particular kind of diagram. But not all illustrations are equally successful. The diagram produced by the statistician, geographer or sociologist can convey a great deal of information in an interesting way but may lack the graphic distinction which a designer would give. And, conversely, the diagram produced by the designer may have all the current graphic cliches but fail in the aim of getting over information clearly and accurately."

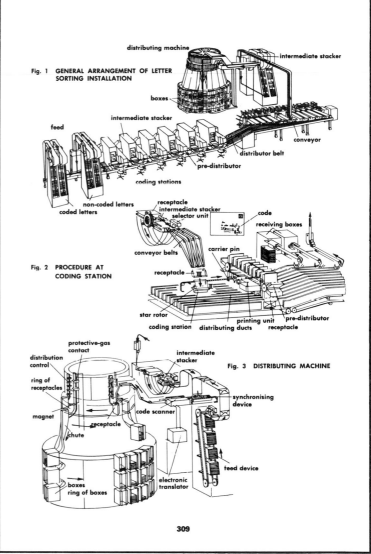

4

The voyages of Columbus.

- · - · - Columbus' 1ˢᵗ voyage 1492 3
- - - - Columbus' 2ⁿᵈ voyage 1493 6
- · · · · · Columbus' 3ʳᵈ voyage 1498
- ———— Columbus' 4ᵗʰ voyage 1502 4

Diagrams
Arthur Lockwood
1969
144 pp
8 3/8" x 10 3/4"
$15.00
Watson-Guptill Publications
165 West 46th Street
New York, New York 10036

This book is a technical reference for the inquisitive. Machines and processes are grouped according to the underlying principles on which they are based. Each is explained in drawings and text. The book covers a complete selection of everyday technology . . .light bulbs, zippers, automobiles . . .as well as an extensive selection of industrial processes.

The Way Things Work
1967
590 pp
5 1/2" x 8 1/4"
$9.95
Simon and Schuster
630 Fifth Avenue
New York, New York 10020

The automobile – number one means of travel

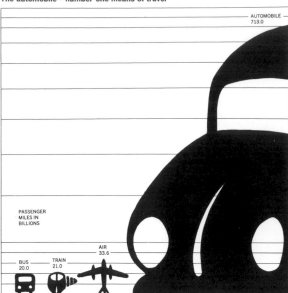

AUTOMOBILE
713.0

PASSENGER
MILES IN
BILLIONS

AIR
33.6

BUS
20.0

TRAIN
21.0

76

In all but a handful of large cities, the automobile now accounts for more than 85% of all travel within a metropolitan area.

In 1962, there were 78 million registered motor vehicles. Counting trips to and from work, driving "for pleasure" and all other reasons for using a car, Americans drove 713 billion passenger miles that year.

In 1964, there were 86 million vehicle registrations. In that year, there was one car registered for each 2.8 persons. According to present projections, by 1980 there will be one registered private car for every 2.4 persons, and total car registrations are expected to reach 120 million.

77

The burden of recreation is close to City Hall

150

3 OUT OF 4
AMERICANS
GO NO MORE
THAN 50 MILES
FROM HOME
TO "GET AWAY"
FOR A DAY

100

50
MILES
FROM
HOME

72

A special Census Bureau study, begun in the summer of 1960, showed that three out of four Americans went no more than fifty miles from home to get "away" for a day. The greatest pressures for recreation demand are not in the wide-open spaces, or even the medium-open spaces, but in what could be called the fifty-mile "day-trip" zone.

Out-of-town parks, with rare exceptions, are not accessible to central city people without automobiles. That means that minority groups, the old and the indigent crowd what recreational facilities are close-by.

73

This is an excellent example of what each city should have—its own visual, easily understandable chart or data book. This one was produced for the Urban America Conference in Washington in 1967. Politicians should see the value of distributing a booklet establishing their concern for making public information public during a campaign and for being identified with both that concern and with the position of being knowledgeable about urban data.

Chart Book
Urban America, Inc.
1967
96 pp
8 3/4" x 8 3/4"
$1.00
National Urban Coalition
2100 M Street N.W.
Washington, D. C. 20037

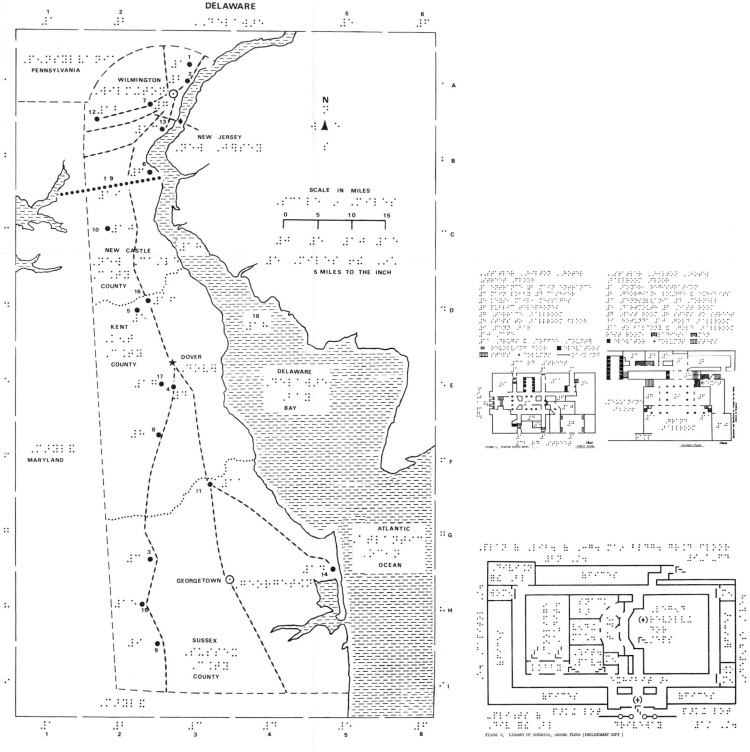

FIGURE 3, LIBRARY OF CONGRESS, GROUND FLOOR (PRELIMINARY COPY)

Maps for the blind are almost as old as braille itself, but the amount of effort expended to improve and standardize braille has been far greater than that devoted to other kinds of graphic communication. The first record in this country of a professional cartographer involved in graphics for the blind dates back to only 1958.

The fact that no cartographer has devoted time to maps for the blind does not mean that they were not needed. The demand has been and still is very great though standardized braille fulfills the requirements for embossed verbal communication, the means available for embossed graphic communication, i.e. maps, graphs, and diagrams, are still relatively crude.

This is included to exemplify the concern for special devices to explain the city to the blind, deaf and immobile as well as to those who do not speak or understand the English language.

The Howe Press
Perkins School for the Blind
Watertown, Massachusetts 02172

Tactual Maps for the
Visually Handicapped:
Some Developmental Problems
Joseph W. Wiedel
The Professional Geographer
volume 28, number 3
May 1966
pp 132–139

The School That I'd Like

I believe the actual equipment should be kept to the bare minimum but there should be raw materials in plenty. For example, in the old concept of a gymnasium, dangling ropes suggest you must climb them. Why not provide trees instead?

Judith, 18

Even a slight rearrangement of the room might stir a thought or two. When a shop wants to attract customers, they put on a bright and attractive display. Why couldn't this idea be used in school?

Peter, 15

The system of a certain set of subjects being taught is wrong; instead of, say, a child being taught geography, history and music, why can't that child do a course on making radios or studying tropical fish if he wants to? I have always been interested in engines and how to mind them, but there is unfortunately nothing like this in school.

Robin, 16

The function of a school is presumably to teach its pupils how to enjoy and how to make the best use of the world in which we live. In fact, nearly all the subjects which are taught in schools, however purely 'academic' they may seem, are fundamentally related to man or to his environment, but the relationship is often not obvious. Because what does exist, or has existed, is taught in our schools under the superficial names of 'Geography' or 'History', very little attention is paid to what might exist, and so the benefit of the acquired knowledge is never properly used. For this reason, the first requirement of the teachers in my ideal school, would be that they be interesting as people, and capable of transforming dry knowledge into the art of living.

. . . the main aim of my school would be that the pupils learn how to make best use of (that is, to understand) the world through effective knowledge. This would involve the breakdown of conventional subject disciplines. The new divisions would be more comprehensive; for instance, since more people are interested in themselves and other people, the study of 'Human Lives and Living' would play a large part in the curriculum. It would include psychology, human biology, geography, history and philosophy, besides aspects of human living represented in art such as family relationships in classical Greek drama. As regards the last aspect, drama, the question which the school children would be patiently but persistently asked to consider would be, 'How should I react in a similar situation?' Intimate discussion between small groups of pupils would be encouraged, it goes without saying, so that the fruits of individual work and thought could be collected and united by the children themselves. This method would teach the pupils that outside school life the class-teacher relationship is, fortunately, not a common one.

Elizabeth, 17

I would go around asking the pupils what they would like to be when they grow up and whatever someone has in mind, e.g. a nurse, I would let her work in the laboratories and I would ask the science teacher to help her with her work as much as possible. If a pupil likes a certain sport such as tennis I would ask the P.E. teacher to coach him or her as much as possible and forget useless games like rounders.

Angela, 13

One of the first radical changes I should advocate would be the abolition of colleges of education for teacher training. Teaching would be reorganized on the following basis. Only heads of subject departments and headmasters would receive specialized training at full-time colleges. Other teaching would be a version of conscription, each member of society would be asked to contribute a certain proportion of his time to take a course and teach and educate others in his particular skill. In this way those at places of education would receive fresh information from a variety of people, learning at the same time to accept people with their own enthusiasms and shortcomings. This system would also help ease the shortage of teachers and the constant bickering about wages and hours.

Mary, 16

There should be extensive departments for every possible subject range, and the choices and combinations of subjects should be entirely unrestricted. For example, no pupils would be flatly informed that he or she must study one of the following: music, history or geography. I am quoting this case from my experience. Marvellous it may have been for those few brilliantly gifted musicians, or for those natural historians, or for those to whom geographical features come as easily as breathing. However, geography, music, history and chemistry and physics just are not my gifted subjects. I have very little or no interest in any of them, and about as much ability. The only way high marks can be gained in these unwanted subjects is to learn parrot-fashion all the facts and notes dictated by the member of staff concerned. In my opinion this is pointless and is the worst way of educating any intelligent human being. The sub-

ject should be studied, explored, practiced and experiments should be carried out. It should not be learned just to be recited; it must be understood. If we were not obliged, or rather compelled, to take the subjects which we have no inclination for, we could use the valuable time to supplement that spent on more favourable topics. For this reason I think that, if desired by the individual, he should spend all his time on his chosen subjects and not waste it on those which hold no interest for him. Then fewer subjects could be worked on in greater detail and to a more advanced depth. Of course, the pupil has the choice: either to take several subjects generally, or to specialize in one or two.

Patricia, 15

The School That I'd Like
Edited by Edward Blishen
1969
171 pp
4 1/4" x 7"
$.95
Penguin Books Inc.
7110 Ambassador Road
Baltimore, Maryland 21207

In December, 1967 **The Observer** invited secondary school children to describe "The School That I'd Like". The response amounted to some half-million words, innumerable charts and drawings. It also amounts to an enormous, good humored, earnest, and intelligent plea for a new order in schools. A pervasive radical note is steady, reasonable, and supported by specific instances. The comments organized here by category are a remarkably honest and sober collection of complaints, criticisms, and schemes for imaginative innovation.

'Geography in An Urban Age is a one-year, multi-media geography course prepared by the High School Geography Project of the Association of American Geographers, supported by the National Science Foundation.'' Through a series of 6 units, students ''investigate the many reasons why things, people, and events have developed where they are rather than in some other place.'' Students become involved in group activities, role-playing, games, model building, discussions, film strips, recordings, readings, and emphasis is on the development of conceptual thinking, student inquiry and analysis. Units include: 1) Geography of Cities, 2) Manufacturing and Agriculture, 3) Cultural Geography, 4) Political Geography, 5) Habitat and Resources, and 6) Japan.

Much of the Urban Geography Kit is excellent fun and informative. I object to the building block device of the lego type boards which allow for land use in lumps, rather than in the mixed plaid pattern it should be understood as being. This is the problem with many other programs that have exercises describing cities in terms of wooden blocks and sugar cubes to be manipulated.

Geography in an Urban Age
High School Geography Project
1965
Unit 1: Geography of Cities
Students' materials kit
(for two students)
$5.97
Teacher's materials kit
(accommodates 30 students)
$240.00
Macmillan Co.
866 Third Avenue
New York, New York 10022

Contact	Course Title	Place Held in Philadelphia
William Addams University of Pennsylvania	Audit Freshman English classes	University of Pennsylvania
Dr. Humphrey Tomkins Director-Freshman English	Audit Freshman English classes	University of Pennsylvania
Peter Arfae	History of Architecture	26 South 20th Street
Richard Ash Plaza Apartments	The Law and You	Plaza Apartments 18th and The Parkway
Mrs. E. Ballard, Director, with Steve Cooper Julie Morris Pennsylvania Horticultural Society	Green in City	Pennsylvania Horticultural Society 325 Walnut
Bob Brinkley	Sound Tape Work	Board of Education Building
Winnie Binkley Spring Garden Community Center	Day Care	Spring Garden Community Center
Mrs. Bobrowicz	Weaving	Nesbitt Hall Textile Room Drexel University 34th and Market
Jean Bockenhauer	Cooking	121 N. Lambert Street
Ron Bond	Swimming	Hutchinson Gym 33rd and Chancellor
Mrs. J. Bonner	Music Appreciation	4047 Pine
Betty Bromnick	Adult Basic Education	Location undetermined
Douglas Brown	Physics	Science Resource Center
H. Brownstein	Economics	Houston Hall University of Pennsylvania
Andrea Burns Carolyn Snyder	Project Learn	Epiphany Church Carpenter Lane and Lincoln Drive
Laurie Burstein Peter Berger (students)	The Individual and the Collective Staff	4000 Pine Street
Gene Castellano	The Written Word	1700 Pine Street
Donna Cavallaro Andy Scherer Betsy Pelcrift	Psychology	Experimental College University of Pennsylvania 4000 Pine Evans House
Fran Ciurlino Tyler Student	Design College	Swedenborgian Church
Leon Cohen Board of Education Division of Art Education	School Art League	Location undetermined
Henry George School of Economics	Economics	413 South 10th Street
Barbara Crocken Philadelphia Services to Parent and Children	Social Working Course	Location undetermined
Howard Dalton	Teaching Reading	Stetson Jr. High School Allegheny and B Street
Nancy Daniels	Personality and Adjustment Fundamentals of Communication	Location undetermined
Mrs. Ida Davis	Modeling, Sewing Designing Clothes	West Philadelphia Group 4601 Spruce
Bill Davol WIP	WIP – Radio	WIP 19th and Walnut
John Donne	Communication Experience	Paxson 3rd Floor
Dr. Edenbaum and staff	Audit Freshman English class	Temple University
Dr. Elkins University of Pennsylvania Medical School	Laboratory Technician	Location undetermined
Dr. Ezikiel Einstein Medical Center (North)	Science	Einstein Medical Center
Carl Feldbaum Assistant District Attorney	Constitutional Rights and Reality	Paxson Room 105
Fleisher Art Memorial	Art Courses	715 Catherine
Susan Gallagher Penn Graduate Student	Survey of Language in Society	47 Springfield Avenue
Miss Tara Glass Mrs. M. Oravetz	Art and History	Philadelphia Art Museum
Mrs. Alvia Golden Lane, Golden, Phillips Advertising, Inc.	Advertising	1737 Chestnut Street 7th Floor
M. Gorsky	Teen Arts Council	YMHA Broad and Pine
Charles Gray Sally Connolly	Learn by Teaching	Children's TV Workshop 3236 North Broad
Terry Hatcher GLCA student	Basic Drawing	Swedenborgian Church

The Parkway Program, Philadelphia's "School without walls," is an innovative program of public education for high school students, and in Philadelphia provides one of the few alternatives to a regular public high school. It now includes 540 students divided equally into 3 units or "communities," each with its own staff and headquarters at different locations in the city. The program is open to any student who submits his name and parent's signature; students are then chosen by public lottery from all eight Philadelphia school districts.

Conceived originally by Cliff Brenner, the Parkway Program was put into operation in February 1969 by John Bremer, director until June 1970. The program is based on the idea that the city—any city—is a vast resource for learning and that education takes place in many places other than the classroom. Courses, class space, and activities come from city resources: businesses, cultural centers, public services, craftsmen and industry.

Contact	Course Title	Place Held in Philadelphia
Art Hauptman, Swarthmore College	Economic issues and problems	Paxson Room 105
Ilsa Hutkin	Creative Conceptual Conjecture	4032 Spruce
Mrs. Barbara Johnson	Games, Simulations	Friends Meeting House 20 South 12th
Victor Johnson, Young Great Society	Arts and Architecture	Location undetermined
Jane D. Kent, Day School	Early Childhood Development	2218 Lombard Street
Mrs. Johnson		
Sol Kessler, Kessler's Supply Store	Retail Merchant and Management	1216 Girard Avenue
Seymour Kronblum	Social Policy and Political Action Among the Aged	401 South Broad Street
Mrs. C. Kalick, Counselor, Planned Parenthood	Sex Education Social Relationships	Art Alliance 251 South 18th
Michael Kean	Hemingway: The Man and the Myth	Board of Education Room 207
David King	General Chemistry Experimental Chemistry	University of Pennsylvania
Nancy Kirby, Planned Parenthood	Human Sexuality and/or Advice	1400 Spruce Street
Oscar Knade, Inten. Learning Center	Child Development and Innovation	5th and Luzerne 6th Floor
Jeanne Kyle	Ideas in Advanced Math	2040 Cherry Street
Randy Libros	International Simulations	1801 Market
Cindy Locke, Sharon Frant, Bob Friar	Theatre Arts	4000 Pine Street
Dick Lewis	General Math	2530 Waverly
Betsy Longstreth, Longstreth Elementary School	Volunteer Program	1400 Spruce Street
	Intern Program	Franklin Institute
Bob Loudin, Director, KYW-TV	Television Work-Study	KYW 1619 Walnut
Lisa Lyons	Topics in Ancient History	3900 Spruce University of Pennsylvania
Lisa Lyons	Tutoring all subjects S.A.T. prep	2101 Chestnut
Miss Mariset, Mrs. Smith, Hartranst Corp.	Infant Stimulation	Day Care Center across from Hartranst 911 West Boston
Jill Marti, Producer, Betty Hughes Show WCAU-TV	Why is TV Such a Mouthwash?	WCAU City Line Avenue
Bruce Maryanoff	Chemistry II	2040 Cherry Street
Mrs. McAdams	Infant Stimulation	YWCA 20th and Chestnut
Lynn McElroy, Westchester State College-student	American Counter Culture and Cosmology	2040 Cherry Street
Bridge McKey, Friends Peace Comm.	Nonviolence, Revolution and Power	Friends Peace Comm. 1620 Race Street
E. Matthew Miller	Semantics	307 S. 3rd Street down steps
Mrs. Moultrie	Afro-American Art and Culture	Stoddart Fleisher Jr. High School 13th and Green
Gretchen Neidermayer, Committee of 70	Municipal Affairs	1420 Walnut Street Suite 910
Carolyn Namiroff, Leaves of Grass Nursery School	Observation of pre-school children	1727 Pine
Santos Narvaez, Training Department Gaudenzia House	Outreach 1	Gaudenzia House 1834 W. Tioga Street
John Packel, Defenders Association of Philadelphia	Experience in law office	Defenders Association 1526 Chestnut Street
Registrar, Philadelphia College of Art	Studio Classes	Philadelphia College of Art Broad and Pine
Cathy Raymond, University Student	Algebra I	3900 Spruce Street
Richelle Reitenberg	Spanish I	1st Presbyterian Church 21st and Walnut
Ed Richardson, Director, Systems Planning and Development	Games Computers Play	Board of Education Administration Building
Dr. Roberts, Mrs. Davis, Hall Mercer Pennsylvania Hospital	Tutorial space	Location undetermined

Contact	Course Title	Place Held in Philadelphia
Carolyn Rodia	Consumer Credit	Philadelphia Credit Bureau 1211 Chestnut Street
Landon Rose	Auto Mechanics	3301 Cherry Street Cherry Street Garage
Harry Sautter, James Pinkney, Bob Limerick	Applied Advanced Electricity	Philadelphia Gas Works 1800 North 9th Street
Harry Sautter, James Pinkney, Bob Limerick	Basic Electricity	Philadelphia Gas Works 1800 North 9th Street
Mr. Schulman	Court Reporting	Location undetermined
Bob Seely	Draft Counseling	Central Committee for Conscientious Objectors 2016 Walnut Street
Dr. Shubin, Center City Hospital	What Goes on in a Hospital	19th and Pine
George Singleton, Institute of Afro-Asian Studies, Temple University	Audit classes 1) Black Experience 2) Black Literature 3) Afro-American Liberation Troubles 4) African Nationalism 5) Pan Africanism 6) Great Powers in Africa	Temple University 1900 Park Mall
Bradley Smith, Tyler School of Art	Temple Talent Workshop	Tyler School of Art
William Smyser, Retired Foreign Service Officer	U.S. and World Affairs	Art Alliance 251 South 18th Street
Mrs. Dorothy Stewart, Miss Anna Glacken, Mrs. Bernadette Jones, Mrs. Susan Schmehl	Home Economics 1401 Arch	Philadelphia Gas Works 1401 Arch Home Service Station
Nancy Stiles	Beginning French	1637 Race Street
Lisa Strick	Communications	Resource Center Franklin Institute
Kippy Stroud, Beth Kron, Michael Shelton	Graphic Design and Silkscreen Printing	Spring Garden Community Services Center 1812 Green
Melvina Taiz, Dance Instructor, Parkway House	Creative Dance	Weightman Hall University of Pennsylvania
Mrs. Termini, Language Staff, Magnet School of Languages, South Philadelphia High School	Language Courses	South Philadelphia High School
Jim Thomson	Architecture	705 North 25th Street
Philip Trachtman, Dean, Philadelphia Institute of Art	Studio classes	Philadelphia Institute of Art 125 South 9th Street
John Troxell, Nancy Santamaria	Language I	Philadelphia College of Art
Le Anh Tu	Culture of Revolution in SE Asia	1736 Naudain
Hanna Waldman	Gemology	Location undetermined
Susan Walton, Community Worker, Christ Church Center	Work study at Christ Church Tutoring Program	1520 Green
Mrs. Webb, Cramp Elementary School	Teaching Reading	Howard and Ontario
Reg Weatherby	Social Problems A Militant Awareness	Experimental College University of Pennsylvania 4000 Pine Street
Mark Weisman	Germantown Community Involvement	Suite 509 916 E. Chelten
Barbara Wilson, Carol Drobeck, Moore College, Interns, Photography Dept.	Photography	1801 Market
George Wilson, Model Cities College Placement	Understanding of College Placement Procedures and Office Operations	1603 Columbia
WHYY-TV, Art Wolf	Television and Film Proc.	Channel 12 46th and Market
John Zeh	Alternatives in Journalism Media and Message	Franklin Institute Resource Center
John Zaccaria, Share Time, Bok High School	Variety of Vocational Courses	Location undetermined
Rae Zielin, Institutional Coordinator, Parkway Program	How to Get a Job	Franklin Institute Little Theatre

This is a partial list of current resource options from which the students of the Parkway Program choose their curricula. As you can see, they are taught all over the city by many talents.

Basically people telling other people what and why they're doing what they're doing and where they're doing it.

Ideally this would be a pervasive commitment of the entire citizenry.

Ideally it would be people who don't know they are teachers holding conversations with people who don't know they are students about their mutual concerns in places where the "show and tell" is the city.

Parkway Program
The School District of Philadelphia
c/o Franklin Institute
20th and the Parkway
Philadelphia, Pennsylvania 19103

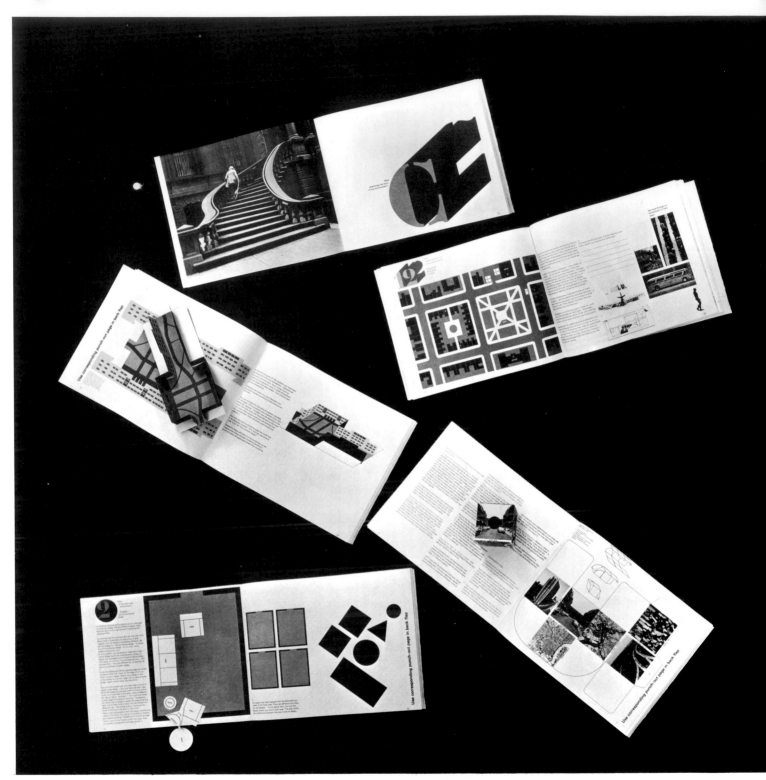

The Group for Environmental Education—GEE!, a non-profit corporation, was started a couple of years ago in Philadelphia by Alan Levy, Bill Chapman and Richard Saul Wurman. Their goals and aims were several:
1. To make the child aware of his man-made environment, aware that it was, or should be, a response to his needs, and that man was responsible for creating it . . . to help him become able to identify and subsequently communicate the elements that made up the man-made environment.
2. To create in the student confidence in making his own judgments and to enable him to develop the criteria that might be used in the evaluation or creation of his own environment.
3. To give him greater aspirations, to broaden his alternatives, to help him reach beyond the limits of his immediate world.

The group's intentions were to motivate the child and to insure his direct participation through problem-solving. Toward these ends the program proceeded along two parallel paths: teacher training and the development of resource materials.

They found that teachers had to be made confident in their ability to handle the program. GEE! sought to provide teachers with a solid framework, a basic introduction into the subject as well as the benefit of other teachers' experiences.

To provide the jumping off point, an invitation to the program, and a basic introduction, a workbook was produced: **Our Man-Made Environment: Book 7**

**Our Man-Made Environment
Book 7**
Alan Levy, William B. Chapman
and Richard Saul Wurman
1970
80 pp plus 10 diecut sheets
11 1/2'' x 9 1/2''

Price varies from $4.75 each
plus postage for 1—4 copies to
$1.50 each plus postage for
50 copies or more.

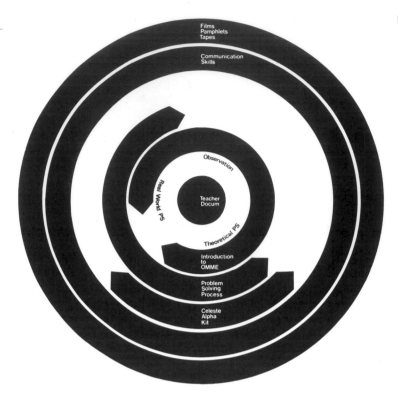

left:

Any program is the man-made environment must be learned through activities. These activities will most likely relate to one of these three broad categories:
1. Observation and communication (learning from one's own environment through mapping, photographing, interviewing, etc.)
2. Theoretical problem-solving
3. Real world problem-solving
Activities in these general categories can occur sequentially, irregularly or in any way that works.

right:

Our Man-Made Environment:
Book 8 is a book about the process of environmental change. It is intended as a supporting resource to a problem-solving activity whether real or theoretical. **Book 7** concludes with the concept of change; **Book 8** is entirely concerned with understanding our role in effecting change. It tries to reveal the components of the process, the way they relate, not as change occurs mysteriously in real life, but as it must be seen to be understood so that the mystery will no longer obstruct understanding. It directs us to question the things we take for granted, such as the kind of environment we want—or say we want; such as what resources we have available and our need to understand, to face up to our priorities; who are the "they" that write the rules that restrict environmental change and what would we do in their place. But, most important, it asks us to face up to the fact that to get something, somewhere, we usually must be willing to trade-off something. The lack of something to trade-off, the absence of an alternative, is the ghetto.

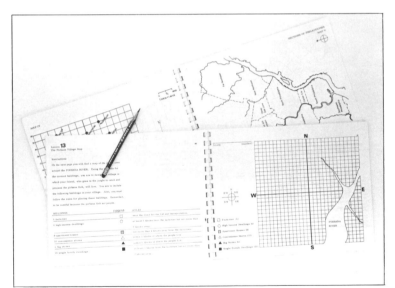

left:

Learning to Get Around
Urban Environmental
Mapping Unit
The Urban Environment
Collaborative
School District of Philadelphia
Pennsylvania Advancement School
1971
79 pp plus maps
11" x 8 1/2"
available soon
Group for Environmental
Education, Inc.
1214 Arch Street
Philadelphia, Pennsylvania 19107

Following a pre-test in 1968 Book 7 was published in Spring 1969. It is organized as a series of problems in response to basic questions:
1. What is the man-made environment?
2. Why do we build it?
3. What are the factors that influence it?
4. How do we change it?
There is also a supporting document for teachers; a how-to-do-it guide which sets down general and specific objectives and describes each problem in detail. It describes classroom activities such as field trips, mapping, and model building, which though related to the book are actually self-sufficient.

In the Spring of 1969 7,000 children took part in a test-program in the Philadelphia schools. This was followed by teacher seminars in Houston, Columbus, Newark, Delaware and seven districts in New Jersey. Through individual meetings and correspondence many other schools have become involved.

Over 20,000 students have received copies of the workbooks to date. They include grades 4 through 9 and some college freshmen as well, and are taught with a variety of subjects such as social studies, art, English, math and science.

Working with teachers involves workshops, seminars, follow-up conferences and most important the dissemination of curricula ideas and activities developed by the teachers involved. One such association with a group of Philadelphia teachers resulted in five classroom programs, written by them, ranging from mapping through pollution.

71

This idea of advising, cooperating with and learning from teachers must be advanced along with the development of new resource materials. The last two workbooks of the 7-8-9 cycle are now in preparation as well as other activity oriented materials seen as important supporting materials in communications, theoretical and real world problems and research techniques.

Efforts are now being made to expand the program into the elementary grades using the school building, the classroom itself, as well as the immediate environs of the school as a laboratory.

Exercises and materials that help the city to become observable give its citizens another incredibly abundant gift—that of an unlimited curriculum as the city becomes an environment for learning.

**Our Man-Made Environment
Book 8**
available soon
Group for Environmental
Education, Inc.
1214 Arch Street
Philadelphia
Pennsylvania 19107

Developed by Coca Cola, this teaching kit has three purposes:

"First, to help children become more aware of their environment; second, to help children to appreciate their interdependence with their environment; and third, to help children realize that, as human beings, they can make decisions which will affect their environment for better or worse.

The exercises involve the children in discussion and debate, and encourage them to make independent decisions about the world in which they live."

The corporate gesture here is exemplary. Coca Cola, perhaps, is reacting to the major fuss now current, concerning their no deposit—no return bottles. The drawings, particularly in the large playing board, resemble a cartoon of the way adults think children would like adults to draw, rather than the more informative tool for playing the game that could have been produced to hold greater interest for children.

Man in His Environment
A classroom ecology kit
1970
Free to school boards from local participating bottlers
The Coca Cola Company
P.O. Drawer 1734
Atlanta, Georgia 30301

Infants may not experience or comprehend the city as such, but they actively develop the foundations of the intellect which in later life patterns or at least influences this comprehension. Indeed, the preception, schematization and general comprehension of the form, organization and functional potential of the physical environment may be more easily assisted in infancy and early childhood than in later life. Through direct physical experience the infant builds the cognitive foundations for the more abstract knowledge of urban form and space of his later years.

The consequences of the perceptions of infancy on an adults orientation in, and comprehension of, the city may be significant. Yet, the environmental learning of infants has not been adequately considered by existing disciplines.

The Infant Learning Landscape to be installed at the Durham Child Development Center in Philadelphia has been designed to facilitate the care and development of fifteen infants under eighteen months of age. This highly symbolic, clearly articulated yet meaningfully organized, three-dimensional playscape has been designed to provide the sensorimotor learning style of the infant with a physical setting in which distinct and significant visual forms are reinforced by sound, touch and color and carefully related spatially to provide symbolically meaningful sequences of experience. The symbolic elements of this learning playscape are of an archetypal character providing forms symbolic of nature (river, plain, tree, mountain, cave) and the man-made environment (house, wall, road, tower, bridge). Appropriately scaled three-dimensional representations of these images are carefully differentiated and related or juxtaposed spatially for maximum clarity and significance. They are organized to reflect

later experience in the world at large (work, travel, recreation, socialization, individual achievement) in appropriate physical surroundings (city, country, sociopetal and sociofugal spaces). In particular, an open box with a roof (house) is situated in an enclosure (fence, wall, boundary) with gates, openings and stored toys (artifacts, industry) which the infant may freely explore. A hard surfaced road leads from this enclosure (city surrogate), forks at a sign post before passing under a bridge to arrive at a natural glade (country surrogate) containing a soft grass-like area (field, marsh) bordering a very flat, winding water table (river) feeding into the bottom of a "tree." Back at the fork the road rises by steps to the base of a ball (bell) tower (flag, maypole, man) atop a mound (centrifugal form) all reinforcing and encouraging ascent, individual achievement, physical effort and verticality. The opposite fork ramps down into a round well, hearth-like, centripetal chamber topped by a dome, a mystical cave symbolizing and fostering shared experience, mystery and passivity. The bridge linking these more or less ceremonial spaces passes by steps from the tower mound but ends in a slide which interjects the enterprising infant into the cave chamber, an initially aggressive, exciting yet ultimately compliant experience.

This entire playscape is carefully scaled to the infant, yet no infant is beyond the reach of adults. It provides the opportunity for an endless spatial odyssey, crawling or toddling through a rich variety of clearly differentiated forms. Individual toy play, exercise, the observation of other infants and socialization of all sorts are also facilitated.

It is hypothesized that the clarity and richness of this environment will help those infants to more

quickly form meaningful schemata about their environment. The important effect on later learning, of early, thorough, mastery of body skills is recognized and will, it is hoped, also be aided (leading perhaps to greater body utility through more immediate recognition of the fit between skill and form).

It is also hoped that such an environment might provide the basis for a deeper understanding and appreciation of both the probabilities and the possibilities, the use and meaning, of later environmental settings. Just as children who have never flown may read aerial photographs on the basis of spatial understandings derived from toy play so children exposed to a coherent, symbolically structured and sensorily reinforced environment at the beginning of their perceptions may become better able to orient themselves in the city, more understanding of architectural and urban form and more demanding with respect to both the richness and the **distinction** of their environment.

All of these spaces and forms are reinforced by appropriate sounds, textures and colors. The cacophonic sounds, geometric forms and hard surfaces of the city surrogate (house, yard, store, work) are differentiated from the melodic, softness, flowing lines and natural movements of the country surrogate (river, marsh, tree, fish pond) while the symbol of individualty, physical prowess and achievement (stair, tower, bridge) are hard against a soft base (mound) while the social, unifying, passive and mystical place (cave, hearth, chamber) is soft against a hard base.

Background Information

An Infant Learning Environment was originally conceived as an individual play/sleep place for the author's children (who grew up faster than it could be made). The design reflects a theory for the coding of visual information which is correlated with a comprehensive information system for design reported on in the **Proceedings of the Second Annual Environmental Design Research Association Conference**, October 1970, Pittsburgh, Pa., John Archea, Charles Eastman, Editors, and in other papers. The entire theory drawing on Piaget, Bruner, Jung, Miller, Simon, Lynch, Norberg-Schultz and others is forthcoming in a book on design linguistics. The immediate work of this project located at the Durham Child Development Center, an inner city unit of the Philadelphia Public School System, originated through the Graduate Program in Community Design, Philadelphia College of Art, a social action program directed, by the author. The school age mothers of the fifteen children who will experience this environment are actively participating in the design and use of the facility as part of their own education in the same building. A developmental psychologist, the infant care staff, representatives of the Pennsylvania State Department of Public Welfare, the administration of the Durham Child Development Center, of the Learning Center and students at the College of Art are also participating.

The Beginning of Observation
in the City
An Infant Learning Landscape
Chuck Burnette
234 South 3rd Street
Philadelphia, Pennsylvania 19106

Towers and building top observatories

"TOWERS was initially presented as an exhibition of 400 photos, 600 slides and 30 models at the Museum of Contemporary Art, Chicago, in September and October of 1969.

"The original exhibition sections of the publication are devoted to:
1. Watch towers — the simplest and most basic type of tower — offering security and knowledge as a function of elevation — a passive information-absorbing unit.

2. Communication towers — active transmitters of information (by means of light, sound, electricity or radio) also providing security or information by virtue of their height.
3. Engineering towers — a survey of towers that perform services for materials. They are unencumbered by human needs. Smokestacks and, for the most part, poles, have not been included since they are virtually simple shafts.
4. Restaurant-Observation-TV towers (Status Towers): Planned to impress the visitor, serve sight seers, or create a landmark.
5. Towers in Architecture — A selection of early 20th Century office towers by Frank Lloyd Wright and Louis Kahn; circular tower buildings; and a grouping of the tallest buildings in the world.
6. Fantastic towers, artist's towers, including many exotic and overtly symbolic concepts make explicit what is implicit in the tower form."

These are some illustrations from an excellent exhibition that is still available from the Museum of Contemporary Art in Chicago. The ability to observe the city from above and the possibility of locating classrooms in the tops of buildings is worth noting. The following pages describe the urban observatory and postulate its location in an area that would allow the use with the ability of a tower from which to see the city.

Towers Exhibition
David Katzive
1969
Museum of Contemporary Art
237 East Ontario
Chicago, Illinois 60611
55 4' x 8' panels
15 3' x 8' panels
rent: approximately $750.00

In 1967 I wrote a proposal for an urban observatory. Simplified, this project called for making public information public. It would appreciably change our city government and practically re-order the current *modus operandi* of our City Planning Commission, Department of Streets, and Department of Public Property.

The institutions and public meeting places in our cities are but extensions, natural extensions, of the street. The street is a necklace of rooms, changing character block by block from the changing demands which interface along its facades. The street is a room with a stupendous ceiling—the sky. Its windows are the windows of all the buildings that frame its space, and the measure of its quality is the measure of the city itself.

The museum of the living city, or the urban observatory, should be the visual data center of the city and region.

Movies and models would describe the growth of the region from the 17th century to the present and postulate ten and twenty-year future growth patterns in population, land coverage, higher education and recreation facilities.

Visitors would be able to "dial" any relationship among these aforementioned elements, even those from the past and thereby understand the various relationships and correlations. Any narration accompanying exhibits on growth should be steeped in the history of the region thus enabling school children to sense the present in an historical context. There should be current maps and models of all kinds describing quickly, clearly, and tangibly things such as houses for sale and their price ranges so that someone moving into or about the city might select a place to live. This might even facilitate open housing. There should be similar displays showing industrial land and plant facilities, their size and cost, the location of the unemployed, substandard housing, personal income levels, tax assessments, and age and population density. There should be listings locating all public amenities, medical facilities, social agencies, etc.

The museum should be a working, educational center for the development of information, where all city plans and proposals for change would first be introduced to the public.

It would ideally be located in the center of the city, and contain the following:

1. On the ground floor, the urban observatory's nucleus.

2. On the second level, a place for activities including a library containing material related to the events of the moment: the city's waiting room, an urban theater of news.
3. Above might be an area that would contain accommodations for special guests of the city.

The observatory should extend a supplemental network throughout the city, with major nodes on the ground floor of all public buildings. Here, city departments would assume their responsibility of describing aspects of the city to its citizens. Through this means the city departments could explain what they do and why they do it.

A city or a region must describe itself to its citizenry. It should do this with enthusiasm, honesty, clarity and humor. Historically, people have chosen to set aside places (now known as museums) for objects and information pertaining to particular phases or aspects of their civilization. Without any doubt, the most significant part of civilization— that which touches all aspects of our lives— is our urbanized environment. In a new kind of museum, the city and its man-made environment with its sociological, economic and political realities should be clearly described to the people living in it. This should be done in a manner allowing everyone to sense the constants of growth and change and the inter-relationships of elements of the community.

The museum of which I speak should embody three major concerns:

formation

situation

aspiration

Formation

Formation is the historical determinant of the region.

Formation includes the form and make-up of the region and the various relationships between political, social, economic, scientific and historical events. Two essential aspects of formation are growth and change, and the concurrent idea of time. Where time is of overriding importance,

Situation is the present condition of the region.

Situation is the annual, seasonal and daily life of the city. It describes what is presently happening in our schools, our people and our institutions. It includes the way we use our money, land, air and water. *Situation* is also concerned with the location of housing types, urban renewal areas and all the movement systems lacing the city.

In this section of the museum, one should be able to "dial" certain relationships: the interrelationship between a highway program and residential development, or a school and the school-age population. The staff of the department of streets and board of education, as well as other city officials, should be invited to use this section to make it a live, working place. This would also be the location of the urban gaming center.

Aspiration embodies future possibilities.

Aspiration embodies the long and short range desires and plans of all institutions and departments of city government. This section of the museum becomes the public forum for the display and public testing of ideas. This display can also educate the public as to what might be, what should be, what could be.

The Place—City Hall

Philadelphia's City Hall, symbolically and functionally the most prominent structure in the city, is centrally located and faces a busy plaza at the crossroads of major vehicular, pedestrian and mass transit routes.

City Hall is owned by the city and based on recent studies, has enormous amounts of unspecified space soon to be available. This building combines the urban spatial characteristics of the Campo di Siena, the governmental symbolism and bulk of the Kremlin, the movement foci of Grand Central Station and the physical prominence of the Eiffel Tower.

An urban museum would fill the enormous gap in public relations and public education now existing in the region, a gap felt strongly by the Chamber of Commerce, the Office of the City Representative and the Philadelphia Industrial Development Corporation. Along with the attraction of valuable people and valuable industry, such a demonstration of awareness by the city would serve to establish once again Philadelphia's leadership in urban thought and development.

Urban Observatory
Richard Saul Wurman
1214 Arch Street
Philadelphia, Pennsylvania 19107

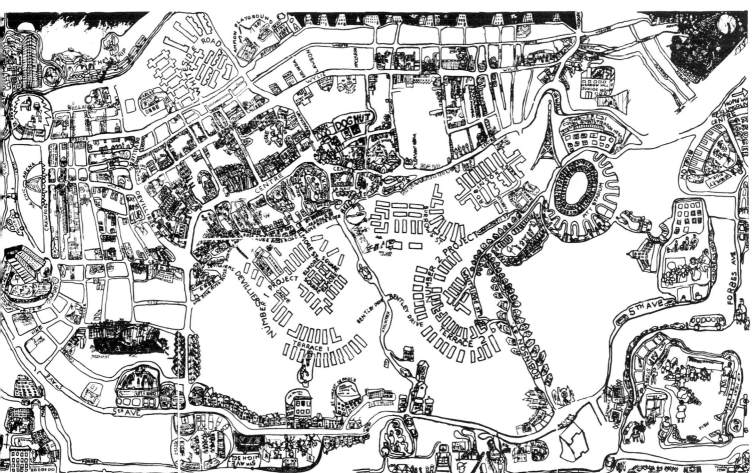

"The problem was to find a way to make a document that people in the community could understand and use in order to participate in the planning and making of their community. It had to be a map that showed how things were in the community and where they could go — like uphill or downhill or tight or strung out. The finished map measures twenty-four feet by forty feet. It is on the floor and people walk on it.

Presently, the map is being used by Community Design Associates to involve its clients in the planning and design of their projects: they use it as a general ground on which to base their decisions. C.D.A. is also using it for a transportation study of the Hill. It has been submitted to Pittsburgh Model Cities for use as a community directory of services and, again, as a general ground on which to base planning decisions."

Why doesn't every community make its own?

This is a marvelous example of what could be the nature of a local map for every community, continuously updated, showing the resources available as well as the location of problem pockets.

Community Map, Hill District, Pittsburgh
1970
25" x 40"
Community Design Associates
2012 Wylie Avenue
Pittsburgh, Pennsylvania 15219

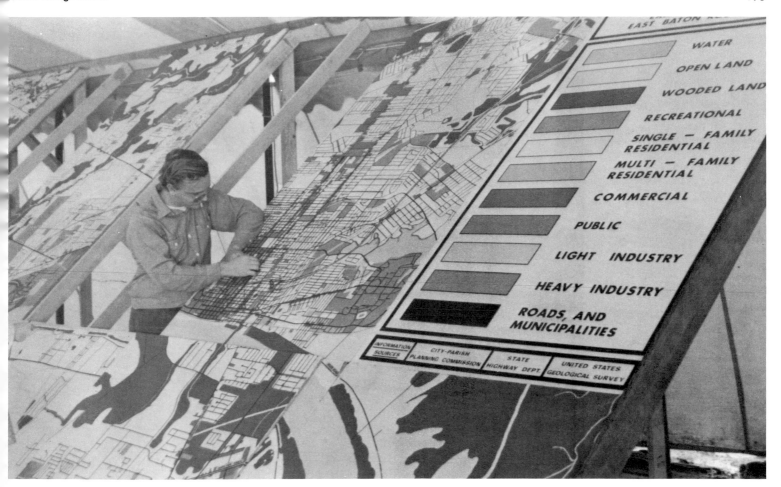

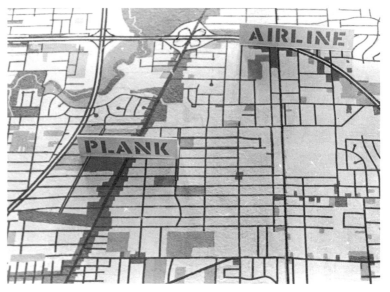

In May 1969, the East Baton Rouge City Parish Beautification Commission began an extensive research effort whose major thrust was the development of effective ways of presenting material about the parish to the general public.

The first step in this program was the presentation of land-use information in an understandable form. A color-coded land-use model, 32' x 32' at 1'' = 400',

was constructed by the staff. Since its completion, it has been used extensively in sessions with mayors, department heads, civic groups, and the general public. The staff continues to develop other visual material such as a color-coded zoning map (12' x 12') and a topography map (8' x 8').

Although the specific technique leaves something to be desired the gesture to the community is very worthwhile. I understand the map is well used and has had a positive effect on the community's understanding of its surroundings.

City Parish Beautification Commission
Box 458
Baton Rouge, Louisiana

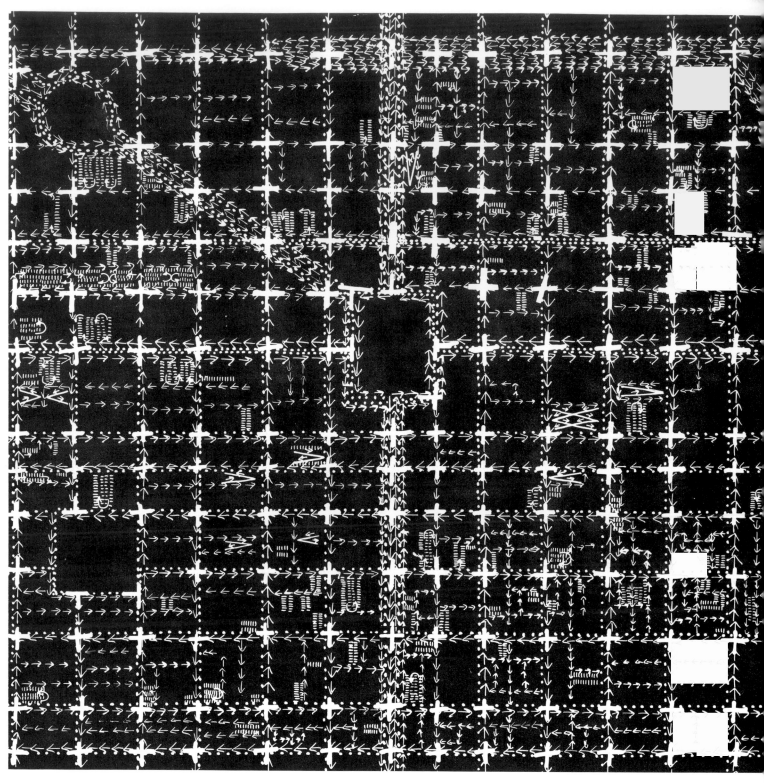

Lou Kahn developed this short-
hand method of showing traffic
movement and vehicles storage.
It remains an evocative exercise
and a lesson in the need to describe complicated information in
a form that allows for understanding and the further development
of ideas. This is a section of one
of a set of drawings, the others
describe the then existing movement pattern.

Louis I. Kahn
1501 Walnut Street
Philadelphia, Pennsylvania 19102

The Notebooks and Drawings
of Louis I. Kahn
edited and designed by
Richard Saul Wurman and
Eugene Feldman
The Falcon Press
1962
75 Drawings
11'' x 15''
$14.50
Wittenborn and Company
1018 Madison Avenue
New York, New York 10021

1. EARTHWORK COSTS

6. INTERFERENCE DURING CONSTRUCTION

2. COMFORT AND SAFETY

7. USER COSTS

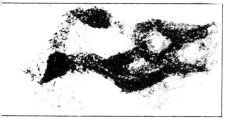

3. REGIONAL DEVELOPMENT

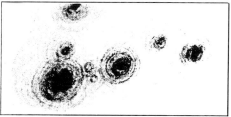

8. SERVICES

4. LOCAL LAND DEVELOPMENT

9. TRAVEL TIME

5. OBSOLESENCE

10. PAVEMENT AND SUBGRADE COSTS

*This important study was pro-
duced nine years ago and is both
a textbook of visual annotation and
a strong case for the use of this
understandable visual technique
in the development of public
issue arguments. This ability to
put together various pieces of
information visually and arrive
at a conclusion developed and
shown visually and understanda-
bly is exemplary.*

"The problem was to locate a
twenty mile stretch of highway
in Massachusetts, starting from
Springfield and ending somewhere near Northhampton. We
defined twenty-six forces which
would influence the location.
Each force seeks a certain kind
of location for the highway. For
example, force number 1, the
need to reduce earth work cost,
seeks a location through the
areas where the land is flat. The
full relational implication of
each force is represented as a
pattern of grays over the terrain:
each point in the pattern is dark
if the force is likely to generate
a highway through that point,
and lighter if it is less likely to
do so."

Several of the twenty-six patterns
are shown here.

"When two or more of these
drawings are superimposed, a new
pattern emerges from the interaction of the individual patterns
. . .Two patterns together may
form certain continuous strands
of darkness, which are not individually present in either of
the individual patterns; and in
the same way, patterns present
in the individual drawings may
be submerged in the combina-
tion of the two."

Alexander, Christopher
From a Set of Forces to a
Form from The Man Made Object
edited by Gyorgy Kepes
1966 George Braziller
New York

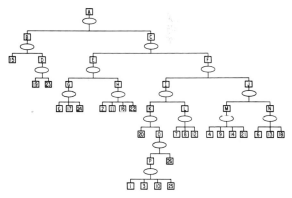

**The Use of Diagrams
in Highway Route Location:
An Experiment**
Christopher Alexander
Marvin L. Mannheim
1962
119 pp
8" x 11"
$3.00
order number PB 194-908
National Technical Center
Operations Division
Springfield, Virginia 22151

9/67

Richard,

I've got an idea for a series of destination films on major cities throughout the world.

Not travelogues or guided tours. A real communication service for passengers from an airline.

If you're on a plane its not usually by choice, but necessity. If the airlines could understand this as well as they do the mechanics of flying——

The in-flight systems can inform as well as entertain.

1/68

Richard,

———a film that feels the way people are in their own habitat———the way they speak—— the jobs they do——the detours that fill out what the tours leave out. After all, the cities we visit are people, not just monuments, museums and restaurants.

5/68

———From the experience on the plane the passenger will know that there is an empathy on the part of the airline for the whole. The film should divert or take the tedium out of a long flight. That doesn't have to be its only purpose———we can come closer to truth in the cliche that you are actually in the country you're headed for the moment you step on to the plane.

Where do the Romans really eat spaghetti after Sunday going to mass———why are the gendarmes carrying those flowers on the left bank———

2/69

Richard,

Other destination films can be shown in-flight to promote the carriers' different ports of call. These same films could be made available to schools, theaters, TV, clubs, travel agents and tourist offices in portable projection units or cassettes.

In addition to in-flight films a total package on board the aircraft would include language brush-up phrases and practice (beginner and advanced) on the earphone system. And a small paperback on the destination, designed to work with the audio-video material. Of course the entirety can become a strong promotion for the airline. It needn't make claims for prettier stewardesses, softer slippers or (?) just-broiled steaks.

The idea has so much to do with why the passenger is on the plane in the first place.

We shouldn't limit the idea to foreign travel. Its needed for intra-continental flights in this country.

9/69

Richard,

———the audio we discussed for the in-flight idea a few months ago could also discuss (in some

detail) information in the guide-notebook. It could also bring local programming from the destination point. It could tell children a story———

12/70

Richard,

I read within the last week that some airlines were going to innovate in their passenger service by having the pilot's and stewardess's occasional speeches spiked with a little copywriting help. Some more description (voice-over) of the topography beneath the plane (to our left the giant firey gizzard creek—). Of course, if you happen to be seated on the right—Have you ever thought about what you would do if you had to use the oxygen apparatus or the emergency exit or the lifejacket (?) under your seat? Its all explained in clear English and other languages in plain view by the nearest stewardess or that card somewhere in the pocket near the vomit bag.

We can present all of this information and more clearly and interestingly on the in-flight equipment.

We can do more than flood the cabin with the scent of mother's breast milk to give the passenger a feeling of security———

9/70

Richard,

Thinking about your ideas on the "observable city" and the City/2 planning. I've seen a relationship to some of my ideas on the presentation of television information.

Primarily the news, weather and other public offerings.

A way to use the medium for itself——why should we look at the radio? Cable television (specifically) is a perfect vehicle for a newer approach to what up until

now has been the province of the magazines. Not a trick or translation of the format but a more visible and understandable use of todays' media to make the city around us more observable.

An inside "look" becomes a restaurant review. Theaters and shops and more are easily presented and analyzed on videotape.

As a primary service function, cable TV reaches the traveler in his hotel room and the inevitable home cable audience with repeated viewings of clearly visualized information as current as today.

1/71

Richard,

Maybe the idea we've been discussing becomes more of a TV guidebook to the city parks, the zoo, the museums, the best way to get to special events, the institutional buildings——the land.

Television can help us to better use the city we live in.

Portraits.

The unglamourous jobs. Whats going on every day that we don't see, right before our eyes.

The Last Cookbook.

What equipment you need, what it looks like, what ingredients you need, what they look like, step by step the way it looks, instant replays, cook it, the finished dish, what it should look like, instant replay, what it should look like on the table, how to serve it.

Make it all available in cassettes.

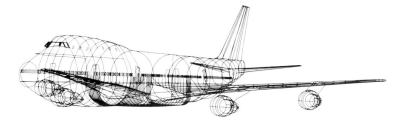

747 by computer
with the assistance
of William Fetter.
See page 29.

Bill and I have been discussing the above issues for some time and these are one side of our verbal doodles.

Excerpts from notes and letters from Bill McCaffery to Richard Wurman 1967 to 1971

William McCaffery
William McCaffery Inc.
1200 Fifth Avenue
New York, New York 10029

and don't forget to vote on the propositions and amendments.

| YES | NO | HUH? |

Next Tuesday, you'll step into the voting booth and they'll be there again–a whole line-up of propositions and amendments you'd swear were written by some Philadelphia lawyer.

You'll read most of them for the first time. You won't be able to figure out half of what they say. And many of you won't bother to vote on them. Or you'll figure it's a safe bet to vote "No" across the board.

Watch out. Sometimes "No" means "Yes."

As if the normal confusion of legal double-talk were not enough, some of the propositions are written backwards. New York's Civilian Review Board and Detroit's fluoridation questions, for example. "No" means "No, I don't want to vote against."

In spite of all this, there is a way to beat the "system." Go to the voting booth informed.

This year, the five ABC Owned Television Stations are again trying to eliminate most of the "Huh's" and "What-do-they-mean-by-that's."

In New York, Chicago, Detroit, Los Angeles and San Francisco, we are continuing until election day to broadcast discussion shows, interviews, news programs, editorials and to make time available for rebuttals so that our millions of viewers can vote more intelligently.

We believe it is part of our responsibility to keep you up-to-date on community problems and suggest solutions. One of our suggestions is that you read the propositions and amendments now.

Here are all of them translated into English for you.

Proposition 1: A Yes vote would allow the State to borrow up to $200 million to buy and develop lands for outdoor recreation, including local and state parks, forest recreation areas, boating facilities, and historic sites. Bonds would be repaid with money from gasoline and motor fuel tax, motor boat licenses, and charges for use of facilities. yes ☐ no ☐

Amendment 1: The New York Job Development Authority makes loans to non-profit corporations to finance new industries and expand existing ones. Money from Authority bonds backed by state credit is loaned at reduced interest rates, but only in areas of critical unemployment. A Yes vote would increase from $50 million to $75 million the amount of state credit the Legislature could authorize to back Authority bonds. yes ☐ no ☐

Amendment 2: A Yes vote would permit the funds from state-guaranteed Authority bonds to be used anywhere in the State whether or not the employment situation is critical. yes ☐ no ☐

Amendment 3: Cities, towns and villages are presently permitted to base the amount of their debts for low rent housing, slum clearance and urban renewal on the assessed valuation of all of the real estate they can tax. (Assessed valuation ranges from 50 to 98% of full value.) A Yes vote will permit them to base their debt on full valuation. yes ☐ no ☐

Amendment 4: A Yes vote would permit the State to loan money to private, non-profit organizations and associations for mental health facilities. The State would be able to use the resources of these organizations. yes ☐ no ☐

Amendment 5: A Yes vote would authorize the Legislature to provide increased pension payments to widows of retired teachers who had been members of the State or New York City retirement systems. yes ☐ no ☐

Amendment 6: A Yes vote would permit citizens to vote after living in the State 3 months (instead of 1 year) and in their county, city or village 3 months (instead of 4). Also, it would permit newly naturalized citizens to vote immediately instead of having to wait 90 days. yes ☐ no ☐

Amendment 7: A Yes vote would allow the State to operate lotteries to raise money to support education. The Legislature would decide how many lotteries to hold, what the conditions are, and how to spend the money. yes ☐ no ☐

Amendment 8: A Yes vote would permit persons away from their counties (or if New York City residents, out of the City) at the time of election registration to be eligible for absentee registration. yes ☐ no ☐

Amendment 9: A Yes vote would allow Buffalo to decide at a local election whether or not the City and its School District should have separate taxing and borrowing powers. This separation would make the school board independent of the city government. The Legislature would determine the amounts the City and school board, separately, could tax and borrow within maximum limits. yes ☐ no ☐

Amendments 10 & 11: A Yes vote on these would permit judges who have reached the retirement age of 70 to continue to serve, when needed, on the State Court of Appeals (Amendment 10) and the Appellate Divisions (Amendment 11) for 2 year periods until the age of 76. yes ☐ no ☐

Question 1: A Yes vote would *prohibit* civilians from serving on a board to review civilian complaints against the Police Department. Only full-time members or administrative employees of the Police Department who have been in the Department for at least one year would be eligible. It would also prohibit the Mayor, Police Commissioner or any City official from authorizing any other investigation or review of civilian complaint. yes ☐ no ☐

ABC Owned Television Stations — abc — WABC-TV, New York; WBKB-TV, Chicago; WXYZ-TV, Detroit; KABC-TV, Los Angeles; KGO-TV, San Francisco

ABC-0/0-210

**The responsible
advertising of
St. Regis**

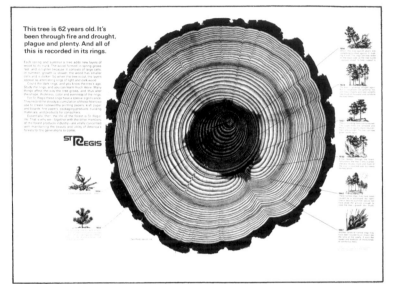

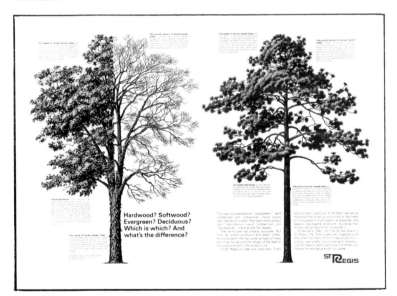

"Five years ago, St. Regis commissioned the first piece of art for a series of advertisements based on the hidden world existing in our woodlands. The campaign was directed toward informing the public about little known and interesting facts of forest life. The criteria set for the illustrations were that each should be accurate, informative, and totally the finest botanical art available."

"We've tried to make our corporate campaign memorable. We want our ads to do two things: Serve the reader by providing him with useful information presented imaginatively. Serve ourselves by strengthening the reader's awareness of St. Regis as a responsible, progressive industry leader."

William R. Adams
President

St. Regis Paper Company
150 East 42nd Street
New York, New York 10017

The series of advertisements was illustrated by Jack J. Kunz, a Swiss designer who works as a specialist on scientific and natural history subjects.

St. Regis did it. They used their advertising budget to describe constructive information about their area of concern.

The Secret Life of the Forest
by Richard M. Ketchum
illustrations by
Jack Kunz
1970
112 pp
8 1/2" x 11"
$7.95
plus postage and handling
American Heritage Press
551 Fifth Avenue
New York, New York

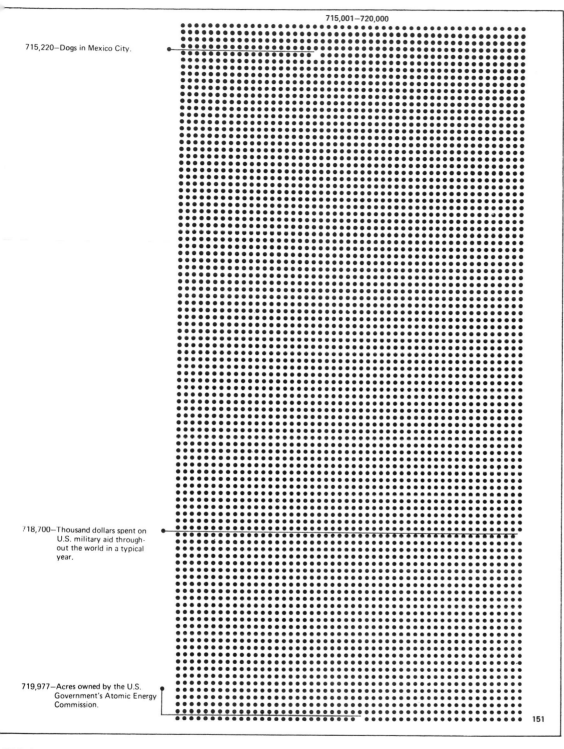

715,001–720,000

715,220—Dogs in Mexico City.

718,700—Thousand dollars spent on U.S. military aid throughout the world in a typical year.

719,977—Acres owned by the U.S. Government's Atomic Energy Commission.

151

FEBRUARY 2, 1971

Business Summary

Lockheed to Take $200 Million Loss In Plane Dispute

Compiled by The Inquirer Staff

BURBANK, Calif. — Lockheed Aircraft said it will accept a $200 million loss on the C-5A transport imposed by the Defense Department as the price of resolving contract disputes.

It also announced tentative agreement to settle its ship construction claims for $62 million.

Lockheed chairman Daniel J. Haughton said the settlements will complete Loc' d's four major contractual disputes over the C' onter, Navy construct ange at

Tax-Sharing Offers $35 Million for City

By **JAMES B. STEELE**
Urban Affairs Writer

Philadelphia could receive as much as $35 million in additional Federal funds if President Nixon's revenue-sharing proposal gains Congressional approval.

The figure is based on several factors including Congressional approval of the full $5 billion "general" revenue-sharing program, a gurantee that would assure the cities of receiving their share, and no cutbacks in existing urban aid programs.

The estimated share, roughly equal to Philadelphia General Hospital's budget last year, would "help," one city official commented.

But he added would not come the

The official contended that Philadelphia could get as much as one-third of the $114 million.

The amount a local government would receive is based on how much revenue it raises in comparison to all cities, counties and townships in the state, he said.

Thus, by a 1967 census of governments, he continued, Philadelphia accounted for about a third of the $934 million in tax and fee revenues generated by cities

This money was supposed to come from three sources: a 10 percent across-the-bar liquor tax was supposed to bring in $14.8 million, but was declared illegal by the State Supreme Court; a commercial real estate levy was designed to raise $13.3 million but late collections have reduced the estimates to about $7 million, and the school board is expecting a repeat of a $15 million special int from the state

'This book is a yardstick, a ruler divided into a million parts instead of a dozen. The reader may use it to measure any quantity between one and one million: it will provide a visual equivalent thereof.

'There are 5,000 dots to a page — 10,000 on each double-page spread. The progression is marked, and a little counting and multiplying will yield the dot that corresponds to any number one ikes.

"The chief value of the book is as an aid to comprehension, and to contemplation. By riffling slowly through its pages, the reader may discover precisely what is meant by one million."

We talk in numbers we can't comprehend about sizes we can't visualize. This book is a revelation to the understanding of what 1,000,000 is. I've included some random samples from a local newspaper. We must use numbers relative to things we understand— to note that we have 1255 policemen holds far less meaning than to say that we have one policeman for each eight city blocks during each shift.

One Million
Hendrick Hertzburg
1970
211 pp
8 1/2" x 11"
$3.95
Simon and Schuster
630 Fifth Avenue
New York, New York 10020

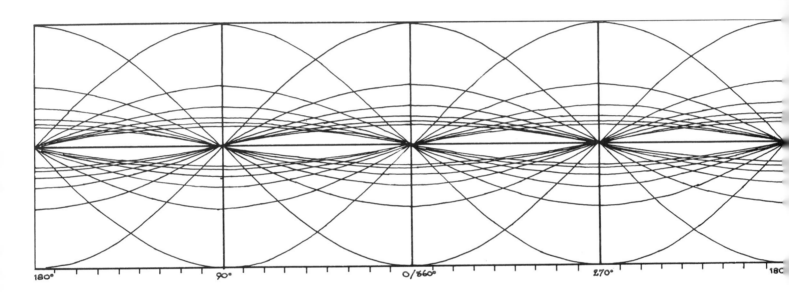

This panoramic photo-montage represents a 360° view of the intersection of Third Avenue and East Twenty-eighth Street, Manhattan. The right and left margins are to the northeast. The camera is set fifteen feet south of the southeast corner. Points of interest include, from left to right, the New York Life Insurance Company tower, the Empire State Building, and in midtown we see, among others, the Pan Am and Chrysler buildings.

A photograph records what was in front of us at a certain time. Perspective is a function of distance and point of view. But one can make the time less certain, the point of view varied. The distance is always a radius, and we can record the inside surface of our sphere.

Part of our ability to design, comprehend and evaluate space is dependent on our ability to describe it. Here are three examples. The system developed by Duncan Stuart is surprisingly simple to actually achieve.

Dave Sagarin
photographer
232 East 26th Street
New York, New York 10010

Wide Angle Perspective Systems
Fred Eichenberger, Duncan Stuart
and James Braden
1970
34 pp
11'' x 8 1/4''
available on request
The School of Design
North Carolina State University
Box 5398
Raleigh, North Carolina 27607

**Panoramic View of the Palace
and Gardens of Versailles**
John Vanderlyn
1814
165' x 11'—12'
43'' strips of canvas
The Metropolitan Museum of Art
New York, New York 10028

Gift of the Senate House Assoc.
Kingston, New York, 1952

The City as a Message System

It is one of the functions of the city to convey information. It has been the custom, in the physical environment to interpret this as a question of products—traffic signs, direction signs, identification signs.

How does the city describe itself and make itself intelligible to visitor and resident. This is a more fundamental question than a choice of type face for a direction sign.

City Hall tower, the river edges, the bridge gateways to the city, the grain of buildings are colossal elements of a ready-made city-wide sign system.

The city-as-a-message-system is a proposal for a life-size route, destination and actual location map of the city—the city itself. (The city of Philadelphia is used as an example here.)

Performance Criteria for the City vs. Rules for Products

The real responsibility of the city is the establishment of performance criteria for the public environment—not for the multitude of individual products contained within the city but for the city itself.

A Life-size Route Map

Inside the city, the street network assumes the role of a guidance system. Elements of the movement system are articulated. Streets assume graphically, spatially and by light, relative status in the movement hierarchy.

The spatial domain of the highway becomes a surface for the presentation of information—route, destination, speed, safety.

Streets Between the Rivers

Routes running between the rivers framing the center city regularly punctuate north-south movement—orientate movement in the downtown, clarify the elements of the street grid, indicate paths to river crossings.

City Edges

Large-scale geographic or man-made features describe the edges and articulate sections of the city.

Identified and given visual recognition, they are signs to destinations, routes—a framework for the visual comprehension of the city.

The Subsconscious Message System of the City

General architectural or spatial events throughout the city, by concentration, become significant or particular to a single area—identify activities, uses, services. They are part of the city dwellers' subsconscious pattern of associations—roof top water tanks and the fringe-downtown manufacturing district, subway stops and the predictability of a shopping concentration above the stop—a subconscious message system giving information about what sort of activities to expect, what sort of services are performed in a particular area—where it is, how to get there.

Where the haphazard mural painting of urban cosmetics would confuse, systematic and insistent color coding would clarify and amplify their power as elements of the sign system.

An Idea for a Three-foot High Wall Along Chestnut Street

Modification of a single street element, the curb, could have positive repercussions in four areas of concern.

Traffic Movement

A continuous three foot high curb-wall along center city sidewalks would eliminate the possibility of parking along the curb except at certain locations—nearside car doors cannot be opened, it is difficult and embarassing to climb the wall. Breaks in the wall would establish bus, taxi, and essential delivery stops. All lanes becoming moving lanes.

Pedestrian Safety

Jaywalking or children straying into the street become next to impossible. No splashing on pedestrians.

Integration of Sidewalk Elements

Trash cans, mail pickup and delivery, telephones, signs, benches and sidewalk vending are taken care of within the fabric of the wall. This does not mean standardization of these elements, simply, giving them a place, a territory within the street environment which neither inhibits their functioning nor allows them to interfere with movement.

Lighting

Use of the wall as a light source—throws light onto the surfaces that require light, from the shortest distance—sidewalk, road surface, the ground floor facade of the street. With lights hung on poles, we are really lighting the tops of cars and people's heads.

An Idea for Alleviating Pain in the Subway System

The system should be comprehensible both above and below the ground—above to identify entrances and routes; below to identify what the stop relates to above ground, a sense of direction and distance.

Distance

Projection of the color spectrum along the tunnel in modules corresponding to city blocks above ground—seen from car windows as a travel-distance clock.

Stops

Projection of the above-ground environment into the subway stations by prisms—the injection of a live sense of orientation and destination, weather, conditions, into the claustrophobia and directionlessness of current stations.

Routes

Use of sidewalk ventilation grills to code routes—north, red; south, orange; west, blue; east, green.

An Idea for Arcading the City

Performance criteria for humane pedestrian domain must include weather protection criteria—protection from wind, rain, snow and sun The creation of a new zoning ordinance could make this possible by encouraging developers to regard the street curb as the building line for all construction above the second floor. This would establish with relative ease a city-wide sidewalk arcade on south and west sides of the street. The additional square footage attainable would be offered as an incentive to developer cooperation.

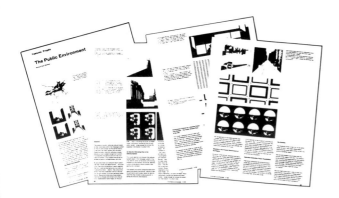

These two articles (only one is here summarized) are heavily illustrated and have many thoughts that parallel DQ 80. The Visual Systems article is in color and constituted a survey of the state of the art several years ago. The PE article is a description of the viable nature of the publicly owned part of the city based on the use of Philadelphia, as a vehicle for description and example.

Public Environment
Richard Saul Wurman
Architecture Canada
160 Eglinton Avenue East
Toronto 12, Ontario
June 1969
pp 43—50

see also
Visual Information Systems
Richard Saul Wurman and
Scott W. Killinger
Architecture Canada
March 1967   pp 37—56

Special subject maps depict national, physical, historical, economic, socio-cultural and administrative characteristics.

Also included is an index of 41,000 place names with geographical coordinates, populations, and other information, and a series of aerial photographs, maps and charts. References are provided to more detailed sources of information.

National Atlas
U.S. Department of the Interior
Geological Survey
1970
355 pp
14'' x 19''
$100.00
Washington Distribution Section
U.S. Geological Survey
1200 South Eads Street
Arlington, Virginia 22202

Midtown Blight is the title of the audio visual presentation prepared for the people of New York City. This slide-tape show is designed to run continuously through the day in a centrally located public space in Midtown Manhattan.

The project developed from the feeling that the incredible vitality of the building boom in New York poses a serious problem to the future of the area.

Midtown Blight
Scott Sebastian and
Elias Vassiliades
4711 Springfield Avenue
Philadelphia, Pennsylvania 19143

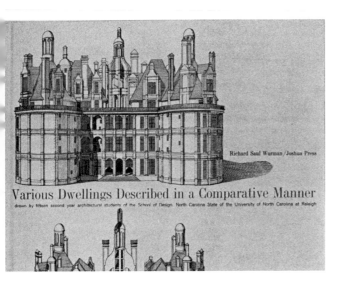

Various Dwellings Described in a Comparative Manner
Richard Saul Wurman and students
1964
64 pp
11'' x 8 1/2''
$6.65
Joshua Press
1214 Arch Street
Philadelphia, Pennsylvania 19107

The compact collection of maps of 46 counties is perhaps the only world travel guide to include so many city maps. Each of these is accompanied by a listing of major landmarks.

New Horizons
Maps of the World
Pan American Airways
1968
334 pp
4'' x 6''
$5.95
Pan American
Pan Am Building
New York, New York 10020

This 26-page booklet was prepared by New York's Landmarks Preservation Commission to help locate 300 New York Landmarks and a dozen historic districts. An alphabetical listing within geographical areas of New York ("Canal to 14th St.", "14th to 59th St.") is included.

The Schaefer Guide to New York Landmarks
1965
32 pp
3 3/4'' x 8 1/2''
free
Landmarks Preservation Commission
Parks, Recreation and Cultural Affairs Administration of the City of New York

These free maps produced in varying quality by various airlines are of much higher quality than any I know that are freely distributed by cities or gasoline companies. I understand the Canadian Pacific Airlines in Canada has particularly fine maps also.

Air Atlas
United Airlines
35'' x 21''
Free
277 Park Avenue
New York, New York 10017

courtesy of New York
Magazine

JANUARY, 1971   VOL. 1, NO. 2

New York
HANDBOOK

Free Health Care: Why Pay an Arm and a Leg?

By Carol Kahn

In his anxiety to get the best care available, the American has developed a costly medical mystique which requires his going to a private practitioner for the simplest procedures. No one wants to crowd out those who need health care and cannot afford to pay for it. But there are also a number of free services such as vaccinations or flu injections which any New Yorker, blue-collar, white-collar, or silk-cravated, can avail himself of in good conscience, if he is not afraid to leave the comfortable but more costly lap of his private physician. Some alternatives available in New York are listed below.

In addition to these facilities, there are many clinics that offer care in specific areas that is not free, but is less costly than its private equivalent. The New York League for the Hard of Hearing (924-3230), for example, gives a complete basic hearing examination for $25, which would cost considerably more from a private physician. And for almost every disease, there is a nonprofit foundation that can provide free counseling and referral. For further informa-tion, call or write the Community Council of Greater New York (225 Park Avenue, N.Y. 10003, 777-5000).

Alcoholism

The Alcohol Clinic, operated jointly by the city and state of New York, provides free counseling and treatment on an out-patient basis to chronic alcoholics or those likely to become so. After getting an appointment, an applicant is extensively interviewed by a psychiatric social worker, who writes up a detailed case history, and is examined by a doctor for physical condition and any necessary medication, such as vitamins or tranquilizers. He is then referred to individual or group therapy. Group therapy currently meets Wednesday evenings from 7 to 8:30 p.m. The Alcohol Clinic is located at 514 49th St., Brooklyn, TR 1-6160.

Alcoholics Anonymous has approximately 500 member groups in New York City. For information, call GR 3-6200 between 10 a.m. and midnight. (Sundays and holidays, noon to 8 p.m.)

Blood

Blood can be obtained "at cost" from the Greater New York Blood Program, in unlimited quantity, for individuals who belong to the program by depositing one pint of blood per year in their blood bank. The Agency

charges a processing fee of $17.50 a pint to hospitals, which is what you as a member will pay for it; hospitals generally charge patients from $30 to $55 a pint. You can also get blood at cost by replacing at the Blood Program the amount you have used. Blue Cross plans offer blood at no charge to members who join their blood program and deposit a pint annually. The Greater New York Blood Program of the Community Blood Council is located at 310 East 67th Street, UN 1-7200.

About 25 per cent of the population possesses rare blood. To supply these persons, particularly in an emergency, the National Rare Blood Club, 164 Fifth Avenue, calls a series of listed donors who will usually drop everything at a moment's notice to donate their matching pints. Service is free to any hospital. The NRBC "hot line" is CH 3-8037.

Cancer Detection

The Department of Health provides full-scale cancer screening for men over 35 and for women over 30 at three locations in the city. The West Side Center has a long waiting list. Call for an appointment: Lower West Side District Health Center, 303 Ninth Avenue, 524-2537; East Harlem District Health

---

IN THIS ISSUE:

Free Health Care

Handyman of the Month: the small contractor

Buying Time: where to find a baby-sitter

Consumer Report Card: Father James J. Gilhooley

A Guide to the Consumer Guides

Luxury Service of the Month: art restoration

NEW YORK   31

New York Magazine is featuring a serialized handbook of services available in New York City. The January 25, 1971 issue is the second entry in the series, and includes 8 pages of information about free (and nominal fee) health care services available in New York, including dental care, birth control, immunization, alcoholism, and weightwatchers, among others. Each item describes the service, who is eligible, the agency name, address, and phone.

Also in this issue are "Where to find a Baby-sitter" and "A Guide to Consumer Guides" both with accompanying complete information on how to obtain the services.

New York—Handbook
1970–1971
Section of New York Magazine
8 1/2" x 11"
$.40 per issue — published weekly
one year subscription $8.00
New York Magazine
NYM Corporation
207 East 32nd Street
New York, New York 10016

1/2 the city belongs to you

If you think all you own is the small plot of land on which your house is built...you couldn't be more wrong. You own more than half your city. You own the streets — the pot-holed streets and the tree-lined parkways...you own City Hall and the corner of 8th and Market. You own the buses and the bus stops...the sidewalks and the parks...the rivers and the expressways.

You own it all — 55 percent of Philadelphia, to be specific — and what that 55 percent looks like and works like reflects your demands and...your indifference.

Maybe you didn't know you owned it all. Now you do.

Maybe you didn't know you could change it. Now you do.

Maybe you don't know how it works and how it could or should be changed. Now you can find out.

The City/2 exhibition

You can see first how your half of the city functions now — the growth and change in your land and public environment...utilities, parking, streets, sidewalks, community facilities, recreation areas, water...all of it.

Then you can see the kind of performances that go on in these facilities — riots, parades, rain, snow, garbage collecting, walking, stickball, traffic jams, shopping — and how they compare with other cities. In special films you will see the action speeded up or slowed down to show patterns of movement you were never aware of before — and how the form of the environment affects the movement of your city.

A third section of the exhibition will show how a change in the design of environment can affect the activities and the way of life. How even the width of a sidewalk can change walking or, for example, how covered arcades can protect from the climate and stimulate business and city life and make a safer city.

And in a fourth area City/2 will display concrete ideas for changing your half of the city to make your life style more what you would like it to be. This portion will also allow for the participation of the viewer, for the recording of his ideas, comments, and criticisms.

City/2 was designed to show urban dwellers what they can demand if they want it, as the articulate demands of the public are the only sensible way to change the form of a city.

You can have a higher standard of performance, a finer quality of life in your city.
Will you start by making the City/2 exhibition happen?

A typical visitor to City/2 at the Museum would see four distinct kinds of communication techniques in use — one for each of the basic divisions of the exhibition.

The first of these subjects the spectator to a highly participatory, highly energized, visually exciting environment. As he moves through the exhibition, the shift in display techniques is from the sensual to the cerebral (from the hot to the cool). The second area is a lively five-screen cinema presentation followed in the third area by a low-key television environment. The final section of the exhibition encourages the spectator to apply the ideas he has absorbed to practical situations. At this stage, instead of receiving information, he has the opportunity to supply his own ideas or criticisms and to judge the projects of designers and architects responding to the challenge of the City/2 idea.

The sequence of spaces in the exhibition moves from simplicity to complexity —
one basic idea,
five movie screens,
twelve television screens,
20 civic urban projects.

Festival of the City

During the six-month period of City/2, the Museum's Department of Urban Outreach will actively bring the message of City/2 to public areas throughout the greater Philadelphia area. People will be encouraged to make something special out of their street. The Museum will also focus attention on street activities that normally occur and inform visitors to the City/2 exhibition of their occurrence. A special media truck will be outfitted as a mobile version of the exhibition. Every two weeks, events will be staged at different locations throughout the city to engage people in community art and environment experiences. Chalk-in drawing festivals, Polaroid photography projects, sound and light programs, and similar events that are both entertaining and eye-opening will be scheduled in coordination with the outreach plans of other agencies.

The street is a community room.

Its design and use must be determined by the people who use it.

The people who use it have responsibility for its design and performance.

The responsibility to determine its use is in the hands of the people who own it.

The people own the streets.

City/2 Exhibition
Murphy Levy Wurman
Architects and Urban Planners
1214 Arch Street
Philadelphia, Pennsylvania 19107
and
The Philadelphia Museum of Art
25th and the Parkway
Philadelphia, Pennsylvania 19103

The Schoolhouse
a self-revealing facility

FROM: GEE! Group for Environmental Education

DATE: 26 October 1970

SUBJECT: Proposal for Urban Guides

We anguish over more school facilities and ignore the unlimited classroom that is our city.

Allowing the city to become observable gives its citizens the incredibly abundant gift of unlimited classrooms and the creation of an environment for learning.

Previously we have ignored the responsibility to describe particular aspects of the city to the public. We should create an invitation to comprehend the growth, scale, statistics, patterning and the aspirations of future plans for our urbanzied world.

An urban guide could be a valuable resource for most teachers. They would see the value of understanding electricity by understanding power distribution in the city, or mathematical concepts by urban statistics or history by the understanding of urban settlements and concentrations.

Exercises and materials that help the city to become observable give its citizens another incredibly abundant gift—that of an unlimited curriculum as the city becomes an environment for learning.

Historically learning has been considered to take place mainly within the classroom and the school building has been regarded as the citadel of truth and the repository of educational procedures.

The most viable facility for learning is held within the elements that make up our urbanized environment and that by allowing them to become comprehensible, observable and understandable, we will then have an unlimited resource. . .a continuous environment for learning.

There are many ways to make the city observable.

The long-term means is to generate the necessary responsibility in the citizenry to make understandable the city's ground floor so that a walk through the city becomes an endless learning experience.

Another and more immediate way to make the city observable is the production of a unique group of urban guides that make the elements of our environment understandable.

These guides would allow the personal environments of the student to become meaningful experiences. His school building should become an environmental laboratory allowing the student to become aware of:

—The arrangement and relation of rooms and a way to analyze them.

—The electrical system and power distribution to the building.

—The corridors and stairways as examples of horizontal and vertical movement systems.

—The water and waste systems explaining where water comes from and where it goes, including ground water and drainage of the school yard.

—The places where social interaction occur.

—The quality of natural light and of artifical light.

—The relation of the school building to the school yard and the immediate neighborhood.

—The materials and method of construction used.

—The teacher environment and areas.

—The student environment and areas.

—The spaces used for Mechanical Equipment—Storage, Eating, Classrooms, Administration.

—As an introduction to land use concepts.

The other series of guides would be on the city itself making the student aware of:

—The determination and patterning of land use based on:

Politics—wards, Congressional districts, etc., Performance, Generative uses, Zoning, Transportation.

—Understanding of controls and regulations.

—Awareness and analysis of the various urban networks: Power,

Sewage, Communications, Movement of all kinds

—The census explored and urban statistics.

—Municipal departments and their responsibilities.

—Community organization and their activities.

The above listings for both series of guides are not meant to be all inclusive.

We suggest that these guides should initially be aimed at the seventh, eighth and ninth grade levels.

The series on the school building in many ways represents a set of concerns paralleling in miniature the groups of urban topics of the other series.

The guides should be devised so that they are generally applicable for any locale with ancillary materials allowing for the development with ease of particular exercises and information directed at specific schools or cities.

FROM: GEE! Group for Environmental Education

DATE: 9 December 1970

SUBJECT: The Schoolhouse as a Laboratory for Environmental Education—as a Self-Revealing Facility

1. We shall select two middle schools in the Philadelphia vicinity for case studies.

2. One shall be representative of an older three-story urban plant with a hard school yard and tight physical relationship to the adjacent community.

3. The other shall be representative of the suburban one-story finger plan with green surrounds, parking, etc.

4. The case studies will specifically show how these two buildings can be made observable, understandable, and useful to the comprehension of our man-made environment. We shall be concerned with representing the various sytems and uses as miniature manifestations of our larger urbanized environment. We shall be concerned with many of the following (no priority intended in the listing—see enclosure memo 26 October 1970):

—Plumbing system—where the water comes from and where it goes
—Electrical system—power distribution
—Corridor—as streets
—Quality of natural light
—Quality of artificial light
—Vertical movement
—Horizontal movement
—Services
—Servicing
—Relation of rooms to each other and to the corridor
—Use patterns over time (a day, a week, etc.)
—Exterior spaces
—Furniture arrangement
—Storage
—Special use rooms
—The car
—The pedestrian
—Entrances
—Communications
—Privacy—noise and visual
—Ventilation
—A day in the life of a student
—A day in the life of a teacher
—Who owns the school building and its equipment
—A day in the life of the janitor
—Safety
—Relation to community
—Where people meet, gather, talk—the social environment
—Costs in running the physical plant
—Costs in constructing the facilities
—Where the monies come from
—Numbers of students

Summary: A six-month project whose end goal is the development (ready for printing) of two distinct products.

A) Two specific case studies describing how two particular school facilities can be made understandable laboratories for environmental education.

B) A workbook kit of resource tools that would enable a school anywhere to describe itself to itself and act as a laboratory in miniature of our man-made environment.

The audiences and participants for these studies would include students, teachers, professionals, para-professionals and architectural students.

Nolli's map of
public places and
spaces in Rome

93

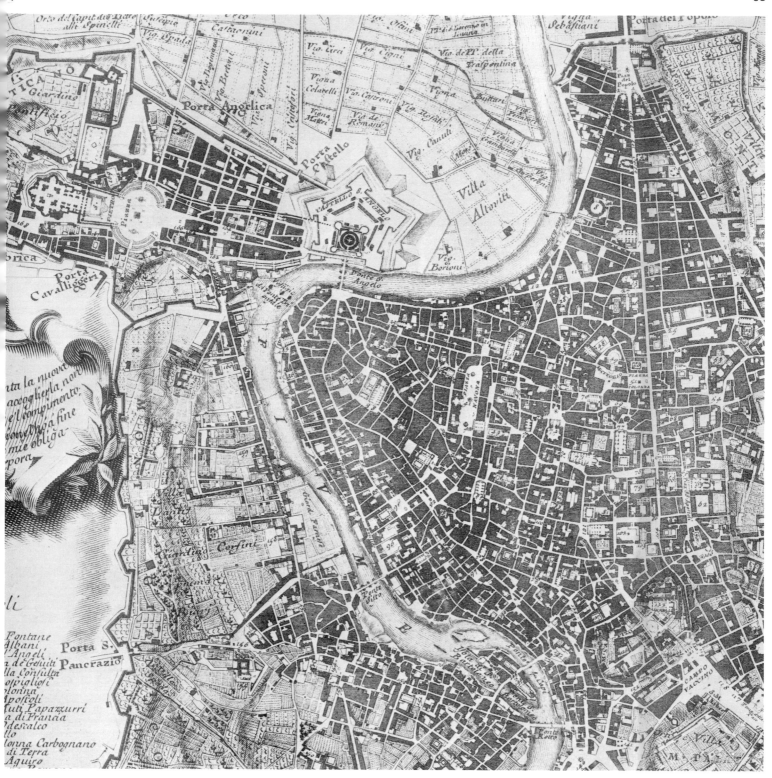

The Nolli map of Rome produced by Giovanni Battista Nolli and his son, Carlo, was drawn between 1736 and 1744. The original is 165 x 187 cm. The plan was drawn with a tinted pen and uses a vertical iconography with a northern, bird's-eye orientation. The monuments, ruins and buildings are all numbered and referred to a descriptive index never completed.

Nolli's plan is a 1748 City/2 display. It describes the public environment of the streets and the ground floor of public buildings in white. It would be exciting to see city maps drawn today in which the ground floor of public buildings and quasi-public lobbies were drawn as a continuation of the streets and sidewalks.

La Pianta d'Roma
Giovanni Battista Nolli
1748
56 x 36 cm
1932
Citta de Vaticano
Biblioteca Apostolica Vaticana

Buildings of the Bay Area
John and Sally Woodbridge
1960
unnumbered
5 3/8'' x 8''
$1.95
Grove Press, Inc.
53 East 11th Street
New York, New York 10003

Seattle Landscape
Victor Steinbrueck
1962
192 pp
7'' x 8 1/2''
$3.95
The University of Washington
Press
Seattle, Washington

Sponsored by the City Council
and the Graham Foundation for
Advanced Studies in the Fine
Arts, this picture guide shows
each of the outstanding structures
of Chicago, with a text by
Carson Webster stating its
important features. It includes
floor plans of original landmark buildings.

Chicago's Famous Buildings
Edited by Arthur Siegel
1965
230 pp
4 5/8'' x 8''
$2.95
University of Chicago Press
Chicago, Illinois 60637

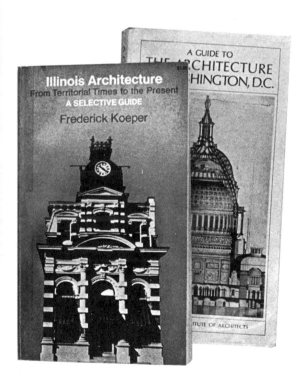

This guide is arranged alphabet-
ically by towns, with accompanying text pointing out the historical
significance of landmark buildings.

"The selections in this book are
intended to convey the history of
architecture as developed in
Illinois. Partiality has been shown
for diverse geographical and
chronological representation as
well as a variety of buildings.
Historical significance has sometimes been a heavy factor in the
selection, but always where the
monument itself was architec-
urally appealing as well. Attention
has been paid to architects whose
contribution is identified with the
growth of the state. Architecture
has always been a single expression
of a many-sided condition; the
social pattern of life, the aesthetic
and emotional response of
environment, the economic and
technological factors — all varying
with the decades — have made
their impact on Illinois architecture."

Illinois Architecture
A Selective Guide
Frederick Koeper
1968
304 pp
4 5/8'' x 8''
$1.95
A Phoenix Book
University of Chicago Press
Chicago, Illinois 60637

Architecture of Washington, D. C.
is a compilation for professional
architects of significant structures, organized into walking and
motoring tours.

**A Guide to the Architecture
of Washington, D. C.**
Washington Metropolitan
Chapter of the AIA
1965
211 pp
4 3/8'' x 8 1/2''
$2.87
AIA Foundation
The Octagon
1799 New York Avenue N. W.
Washington, D. C. 20036

COPE

The environment is now on the ublic mind. Channels to information on environmental education are needed. This collection f sources will only function if we ontinue to have input for better esources. Both additional materials and criticisms of the ones ncluded here are solicited. This uide to environmental education . considered as a working tool o be refined as more becomes nown about this infant subject. he guide attempts to provide a pectrum of viewpoints to suit arious tastes. It makes no ttempt to be inclusive, being nly a body of information ontributed by various knowldgeable individuals and groups.

t is organized in two parts—one or the interested design proessional and the other for his se with educators. While there re a variety of vehicles for pubic education, this one stresses ducation through primary and econdary levels."

A periodical catalogue of educaional resource materials pubished six times a year in two arge catalogues (June and December) and four smaller ones August, October, February, April).

he BRCM also reviews games, ooks, equipment and curricula ideas. Contents include information about process learning, ducational environments, classoom materials and home learning.

SEE

"The materials which we have assembled are a program for building a program. They could also be viewed as a workbook for building a workbook. . .but we hope not. The underlying premise which has guided our efforts in developing the program is that the teacher is in control, that he is in the position of immediate decision making in the classroom and will choose and select not only what will be taught, what will be emphasized, and how it will be taught, but also, but equally important, what kind of atmosphere will exist in the classes. With this prior understanding of the teacher's role, we are not advocating any particular program, lessons or materials. Rather, we are asking only that you plan to include some study of environmental topics in your classes.

If you do not choose to use one of these prepared courses of study, you can make use of many

Big Rock Candy Mountain is the educationally directed spin-off of the Whole Earth Catalogue. As with the earlier effort, listings are uneven, sometimes fresh and exciting but sometimes described so poorly that they preclude curiosity. Their gesture at making information known is exciting and this DQ has felt their influence.

of the ideas contained in this booklet to build your own program. You might take one class period each week for a discussion or activity in an environmental topic, or a week long investigation of some particular local environmental problem. You might carry on a series of group projects in environmental investigation and development, perhaps culminating in actually bringing about positive changes in the community. You might experiment with the classroom or the school building as a model environment, changing it in various ways and discussing the effects of the changes.

Programs of environmental understanding have been introduced in a variety of courses on a variety of levels. Many of the basic goals are the same, but the particular skills which are developed and the difficulty of the tasks presented to the student are adapted to suit the capabilities of the students. English classes have done descriptive writing assignments and research papers on problems in the environment as well as discuss pieces of literature which have application to environmental sensitivities. In social studies, classes have undertaken a variety of activities from reading and discussing books which are addressed to environmental problems to playing environmental games which continue for several weeks. Science classes have devoted time to a study of air and water pollution, conducting laboratory experiments which illustrate the chemistry of certain types of pollutants. Other teachers in a variety of subject areas have found other ways for introducing environmental lessons in their classes including walking tours of a neighborhood, interviews with neighborhood citizens, trips to areas of natural beauty and to areas where redevelopment is taking place. Some classes have made actual presentations to city councils, representing their

SEE and COPE are two recent efforts to develop bibliographies of environmental educational projects, materials and attitudes. Some of the material is listed somewhat indiscriminately. The SEE effort is quite a remarkable project by four AIA Scholars in the summer of 1970 and is continuing through the auspices of the AIA Student Chapters and Bruce Webb. Their views of the state of the art are worth finding out about.

concern for the environment and their desire to do something about improving it. There is an almost boundless variety of things which various schools are trying out. Many have been generated on a local level and have produced enthusiastic reactions from students and teachers.

These materials and programs share many of the same qualities. They have grown up in response to a growing crisis and are directed towards an awakening of sensitivities and sensibilities and a rebuilding of values. They employ activities which build and reinforce skills to assist the student in understanding concepts. Processes are the subject matter, for change is the field of study. Our environment, both the man-made and the natural, is ever-changing. It changes under its own power, usually slowly and gracefully, and it changes more rapidly with the help of man. As it changes it constantly redefines the context in which we live our lives."

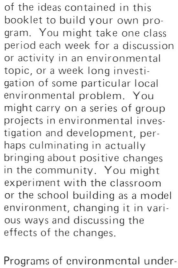

Environmental Education
AIA COPE
Committee on Public Education
1970
3 units
8 1/2" x 11"
out of print
AIA Washington
1785 Massachusetts Avenue N.W.
Washington, D. C. 20036

SEE
Structure for Environmental Education
The Institute Scholars of the AIA
Dan Conrad, Susan Jones,
Janet Null and Bruce Webb
1970
8 1/2" x 11"
Bruce Webb
Vice President, Public Education
Association of Student Chapters
AIA
601 West Main
Bozeman, Montana 59715

Big Rock Candy Mountain
1970
56 pp
10 1/2" x 14 1/2"
$4.00
Big Rock Candy Mountain
1115 Merrill Street
Menlo Park, California 94025

"Men may find God in nature, but when they look at cities, they are viewing themselves."

Paul Ylivsaker
Old Cities and New Towns,
Alvin Schwartz, p. 7.

Doxiadis's Ekistics Center in Athens has model displays at the ekistics scales of towns, cities and regions in Greece. The models can be called for and moved into position by overhead crane.

*The Athens Center of Ekistics
Box 471
Athens, Greece*

Ira Baker has created a Micro Michelin in his Walks for Architects in Chicago.

In the Hansa district of Berlin I understand there is a pavillion of urban information as well as models of the varying districts throughout the city.

In Chicago at the civic center complex and adjacent to the square dominated by the sculpture by Picasso is a miniature in bronze of the sculpture used by the blind.

The Philadelphia City Planning Commission developed a fine map widely distributed of a walking tour through the redeveloped Society Hill Area.

*Philadelphia City Planning Commission
City Hall Annex
13th Floor
Philadelphia, Pennsylvania*

The Philadelphia Panorama exhibit at the Museum of the Civic Center is an outgrowth of a fine public exhibit held at Gimbels in the late forties and marked a rebirth of activities in the city. The Panorama is a collective exhibition including a massive turnover model of the city then, now and perhaps.

*The Museum of the Civic Center
34th and Civic Center Boulevard
Philadelphia, Pennsylvania*

*Open: Tuesday through Saturday
9 AM to 5 PM
Sunday, 1 PM to 5 PM
Tuesday till 10 PM
Closed Monday*

Admission free

The Institute for Advanced Studies in the Fine Arts at MIT and its director Gyorgy Kepes proposed a responsive light and water display for Boston Harbor— responsive to city movement, city information and city sounds.

Richard Saul Wurman, 35, is a partner in the architecture and urban planning firm Murphy Levy Wurman in Philadelphia.

He is among those young architects and planners who give real time to activities related only indirectly to the practice of architecture. His outside involvements, primarily educational, include writing, teaching and the development of exhibitions. Several of his projects are included in this publication.

Mr. Wurman is Vice President of GEE! Group for Environmental Education, Inc., a non-profit corporation developing **Our Man-Made Environment,** a program for secondary schools. He is a board member of the International Design Conference in Aspen. A student and former employee of Louis I. Kahn, Mr. Wurman produced with Gene Feldman **The Notebooks of Louis I. Kahn** in 1963.

Wurman, a graduate of the University of Pennsylvania, received Chandler Fellowships in 1959 and 1968, a Graham Fellowship in 1966 and was a Guggenheim Fellow in 1969.

Currently he is a professor and chairman of the freshman year in architecture at the City College of New York having served previously on the faculties of Princeton University, Cornell University, Cambridge University (England) and the University of North Carolina at Raleigh.

Murphy Levy Wurman, the urban design consultant for the center city waterfront project in Philadelphia called Penn's Landing, has also participated in a wide range of architectural, planning, graphics and interior design projects. They are the developers of a temporary information system for the Philadelphia International Airport and are the planning consultants to the Delaware Port Authority on the route location and station design criteria for the highspeed mass transit network from New Jersey into Philadelphia. Recently they completed the centercity IVB banking space and a series of beach houses in Long Beach Island, New Jersey. Wurman's commitment to the public environment has led to the development of the forthcoming exhibition City/2 at the Philadelphia Museum of Art.

Your comments, questions, corrections and in particular additions and actual materials are invited. I would welcome your responses and I entertain the possibility of an enlarged and more accurate second edition.

Although we have attempted to make information concerning cost and credits exact, we cannot be responsible for difficulties resulting from their inaccuracy. We apologize to individuals we failed to properly credit; most costs given do not include postage or handling. In addition, costs today are not what costs will be tomorrow.

**To give
Design Quarterly
use this order form**

Please send.................issues
of Design Quarterly and a gift
card with my name to the
recipient below. Bill me later.

Donor's name

....

Address

....

City	State	Zip code

Recipient's Name

....

Address

....

City	State	Zip code

**To receive
Design Quarterly
use this order form**

Name

....

Firm name and address

....

Home address

....

City	State	Zip code

check preferred mailing address

☐ New   ☐ 4 issues $5.00

☐ Renewal   ☐ 8 issues $9.25

☐ Payment enclosed   ☐ 12 issues $12.50

☐ Bill me   Rates apply only to the U.S. and
                         Canada. Add $1.00 per year to
                         foreign subscriptions

**To receive
Design Quarterly
use this order form**

Name

....

Firm name and address

....

Home address

....

City	State	Zip code

check preferred mailing address

☐ New   ☐ 4 issues $5.00

☐ Renewal   ☐ 8 issues $9.25

☐ Payment enclosed   ☐ 12 issues $12.50

☐ Bill me   Rates apply only to the U.S. and
                         Canada. Add $1.00 per year to
                         foreign subscriptions

Business Reply Card
No stamp necessary if mailed in the United States

Postage will be paid by

Design Quarterly

Vineland Place
Minneapolis Minnesota 55403

First Class
Permit No. 3626
Minneapolis,
Minnesota

Business Reply Card
No stamp necessary if mailed in the United States

Postage will be paid by

Design Quarterly

Vineland Place
Minneapolis Minnesota 55403

First Class
Permit No. 3626
Minneapolis,
Minnesota

Business Reply Card
No stamp necessary if mailed in the United States

Postage will be paid by

Design Quarterly

Vineland Place
Minneapolis Minnesota 55403

First Class
Permit No. 3626
Minneapolis,
Minnesota